Clear Faith
Eight Simple Truths Every Christian Should Know

The Freeman Institute

FOR INTEGRATIVE RESEARCH

Eric J. Freeman, PhD

The Freeman Institute

FOR INTEGRATIVE RESEARCH

Published by
The Freeman Institute for Integrative Research
201 Columbia Mall Blvd.
Columbia, SC 29223

ISBN 979-8-9929512-0-2

First Edition

The Freeman Institute for Integrative Research

This handbook is a product of *The Freeman Institute for Integrative Research*, an interdisciplinary entity dedicated to examining complex theological and societal issues through multiple academic lenses. The Institute focuses particularly on making doctrine accessible, exploring under-researched topics in theological discourse, and incorporating historically marginalized perspectives that contribute to a more comprehensive understanding of Christian faith and practice.

Through its publications and initiatives, the Institute develops accessible, research-informed resources that bridge theoretical theology with practical application. This handbook on doctrine exemplifies the Institute's commitment to integrating biblical truth with contemporary challenges, providing believers with frameworks that foster both theological fidelity and meaningful spiritual growth in an increasingly complex world.

Table of Contents

CHAPTER 2 ORIGINAL SIN

BORN BROKEN, REDEEMED WHOLE

CHAPTER 3 CANON (SCRIPTURE)

TRUSTING THE STORY, THE RELIABILITY OF GOD'S WORD

CHAPTER 4 THE TRIUNE NATURE OF GOD

GOD WITH US: FATHER, SON, & HOLY SPIRIT

CHAPTER 5 RESURRECTION

LIFE AFTER DEATH, HOPE BEYOND THE GRAVE

CHAPTER 6 INCARNATION

GOD IN FLESH, GOD IN US

CHAPTER 7 NEW CREATION

BORN AGAIN TO LIVE AGAIN

CHAPTER 8 ESCHATOLOGY

LIVING IN LIGHT OF THE END

Preface

Clear Faith, Firm Foundations

Doctrine matters—profoundly. Yet, many believers find the word "doctrine" daunting, assuming it is only for theologians or scholars. But what if doctrine is not meant to complicate our faith, but to clarify it? What if it is not merely abstract knowledge, but a roadmap guiding our everyday journey with Christ?

Doctrine, simply put, is the structured understanding of *what we believe, why we believe it,* and *how we live it.*

This handbook emerged from my personal journey and professional study, deeply influenced by the transformative preaching of Francis James Grimké and my research on Evangelical Emancipatory Homiletics™. I've learned that clear doctrine not only informs our faith but empowers us to live boldly, faithfully, and justly.

Each doctrine explored in this book is central to a flourishing Christian life. These are not merely ideas to be debated—they are truths to be lived, truths that ground us in Christ and fuel our discipleship. Throughout my journey, from my earliest experiences preaching in a small Florida church to academic research and ministry leadership, I've discovered the power of doctrine to change lives, including my own.

In the following pages, we'll explore eight core truths, captured by the acronym D.O.C.T.R.I.N.E.:

- Deity

- Original Sin
- Canon (Scripture)
- Triune Nature
- Resurrection
- Incarnation
- New Creation
- Eschatology

Each doctrine will be presented clearly and succinctly, reinforced by biblical references, and linked to everyday living. Reflection questions will invite you to engage more deeply, transforming doctrinal knowledge into practical wisdom and action.

I am especially grateful for Michael Parker, who began as a student in our college ministry, grew into an intern, and now serves as our chief of staff. Michael invested countless hours interviewing me as we teased out the core structure of this handbook, and his contributions were invaluable.

My prayer is that this handbook will help you lay a firm foundation for your faith, one that withstands life's storms and enables you to grow in grace and truth. May it inspire you to reflect Christ more vividly in your daily interactions and empower you to communicate these life-changing truths to others, bringing clarity and conviction in an age of confusion.

Let's build together on the firm foundation of clear, simple truths.

Introduction

What is D.O.C.T.R.I.N.E.?

✦

Watch your life and doctrine closely. Persevere in them, because if you do, you will save both yourself and your hearers.

1 Timothy 4:16 (NIV)

Have you ever heard a humorous misunderstanding of scripture that, while amusing, revealed a deeper need for clear doctrine? I recall a church member who steadfastly refused to board an airplane. When I inquired about their reluctance, their sincere response was, "Well, Pastor, the Bible says, 'Low, I am with you always.' If Jesus wanted me flying, He'd have said 'high'!" Now, this statement was shared with a twinkle in the eye and a chuckle from those around us, yet beneath the humor was a genuine misunderstanding about God's promise of presence and Christ's deity. Jesus' promise in Matthew 28:20—"Lo, I am with you always"—is an assurance of His constant divine presence, transcending every circumstance, not an altitude restriction for His followers. This playful misconception subtly highlights how essential clarity on doctrines, such as the Deity of Christ, is in shaping our confidence and courage in life's everyday decisions.

On a more serious note, I recall multiple conversations during my pastorate with believers who lived under the anxiety that every time they sinned, they had to "get saved" again. I vividly remember a faithful member who would repeatedly come forward during altar calls (our church's invitation at the end of services for people to respond to the message by coming to the front), tears streaming down her face, earnestly seeking salvation anew. Her deep sincerity was unquestionable; however, her peace was continually disrupted by an ill-informed understanding of what it meant to be a "new creation" in Christ. Her misunderstanding stemmed from an unclear grasp of the doctrine of regeneration— God's gracious work in making us spiritually alive and securing our identity in Christ (2 Corinthians 5:17). Once she gained clarity about the truth that salvation was not a fleeting state but an enduring new identity given by God, her spiritual anxiety transformed into lasting peace and confidence.

These illustrations, both humorous and serious, vividly portray why a clear understanding of doctrine matters deeply. Doctrine isn't simply abstract theology; it impacts our everyday choices, our spiritual confidence, and our understanding of God's active presence in our lives. Clear doctrine provides firm ground beneath our feet, equipping us to live faithfully and fearlessly, whether stepping onto a plane or embracing the freedom and assurance of our salvation.

Defining Doctrine Clearly

Doctrine is not a complicated theological term reserved only for scholars; rather, it is simply core biblical truth clearly understood and practically lived. At its essence, doctrine refers to the foundational teachings of Scripture that form the bedrock of our faith and guide our daily walk with Christ. Far from being abstract or purely academic, doctrine is intensely practical. It shapes not only our beliefs but also our behaviors, influencing how we interact with others, respond to challenges, and experience God in everyday life.

Understanding doctrine clearly equips believers to live faithfully as disciples of Jesus. It helps us discern truth from error, provides stability in uncertain times, and deepens our relationship with God and others. Doctrine serves as the framework upon which genuine Christian discipleship is built—anchoring us in the truth of who God is, who we are in Him, and how we are called to live out our faith each day. As we clarify and internalize these core truths, doctrine becomes a transformative force, guiding our hearts and actions closer to the image and character of Christ.

Introducing D.O.C.T.R.I.N.E.

The acronym D.O.C.T.R.I.N.E., a helpful tool for understanding foundational Christian beliefs, originated from Hank Hanegraaff, president of the Christian Research Institute (CRI), and was popularized through his radio program, "Bible Answer Man." [1] Much like others who've encountered this practical resource, I learned of this acronym during my ministry journey. In fact, as I recall, I first heard it shared by a missionary while lecturing at West African Theological Seminary in Abuja, Nigeria, in 2015.

---

[1] Note: For more information about Hank Hanegraaff's ministry at CRI, visit https://www.equip.org/.

D.O.C.T.R.I.N.E.: Core Christian Truths

Letter	Doctrine & Scripture	Description
D	DEITY John 1:1,14	Jesus is fully God
O	ORIGINAL SIN Romans 5:12	Humanity's brokenness
C	CANON 2 Timothy 3:16-17	Scripture is trustworthy
T	TRIUNE NATURE 2 Cor. 13:14	Father, Son, Spirit
R	RESURRECTION 1 Cor. 15:17-22	Victory over death
I	INCARNATION John 1:14	God became human
N	NEW CREATION 2 Cor. 5:17	Spiritual rebirth
E	ESCHATOLOGY Rev. 21:1-5	Christ's return

Each letter in D.O.C.T.R.I.N.E. stands for a foundational doctrine critical to our understanding and practice of the Christian faith:

- **D – Deity**: Jesus is fully God. Recognizing Christ's divinity anchors our worship, obedience, and assurance of salvation.

- **O – Original Sin**: Humanity's inherent brokenness and our universal need for redemption through Christ's sacrifice.

- **C – Canon (Scripture)**: God's Word is trustworthy, authoritative, and essential for guiding faith and practice.

- **T – Triune Nature of God**: Understanding the mystery and beauty of God as Father, Son, and Holy Spirit, relationally and redemptively engaging with humanity.

- **R – Resurrection**: Christ's victorious resurrection over death provides the cornerstone for our eternal hope and present-day living in victory.

- **I – Incarnation**: God's ultimate act of solidarity and compassion through Jesus Christ becoming fully human to redeem us.

- **N – New Creation**: The transformative reality and ongoing power of being spiritually reborn and continually shaped into Christ's image.

- **E – Eschatology**: Living faithfully and purposefully today in hopeful anticipation of Christ's promised return and His eternal reign.

Together, these doctrines form a cohesive and practical foundation for daily Christian discipleship, providing clarity, confidence, and consistency in our walk with Christ.

Biblical Support

Scripture clearly underscores the necessity and practicality of understanding doctrine. The Canon (Scripture) is foundational because "All Scripture is God-breathed and is useful for teaching, rebuking, correcting and training in righteousness, so that the servant of God may be thoroughly equipped for every good work" (2 Timothy 3:16–17). A clear grasp of Scripture ensures that our decisions, behaviors, and responses to life's challenges align with God's truth rather than cultural norms or personal feelings.

Regarding the Deity and Incarnation of Christ, John 1:1,14 declares, "In the beginning was the Word, and the Word was with God, and the Word was God... The Word became flesh and made his dwelling among us." Affirming Jesus as God incarnate deeply shapes our worship, ethics, and understanding of God's intimacy with humanity.

The doctrines of Original Sin and New Creation remind us of humanity's initial dignity, subsequent fall, and redemptive hope. Genesis 1:26–27 outlines humanity created in God's image, while Romans 5:12 clarifies how sin corrupted that image, necessitating redemption and rebirth (John 3:3–8). Recognizing our need for redemption fosters humility, gratitude, and hope.

The Triune Nature of God is reflected clearly in 2 Corinthians 13:14: "May the grace of the Lord Jesus Christ, and the love of God, and the fellowship of the Holy Spirit be with you all." This relational understanding influences our prayer life, communal living, and our ability to experience and share God's presence.

Paul underscores the significance of the Resurrection in 1 Corinthians 15:17–22, asserting, "If Christ has not been raised, your faith is futile... But Christ has indeed been raised from the dead." The resurrection transforms despair into hope, giving believers courage, purpose, and perseverance even amidst hardship.

Lastly, Eschatology encourages purposeful living and hopeful expectation. Revelation 21:1–5 beautifully depicts the ultimate fulfillment of God's redemptive plan: a new heaven and a new earth where all tears are wiped away. This truth motivates believers toward holy living and active participation in God's mission today.

Real-Life Examples: Grimké & Doctrine in Action

Francis James Grimké serves as a compelling real-life example of how a clear doctrinal foundation powerfully shapes practical actions and social engagement. Born into slavery in the United States, Grimké became a distinguished Presbyterian pastor known for courageously confronting the racial injustices of his time. His steadfast commitment to biblical doctrine profoundly informed his perspective, guiding him to passionately advocate for the equality and dignity of all people.[2]

Grimké's understanding of the Incarnation deeply influenced his ministry. Knowing that Christ fully identified with human suffering and injustice, Grimké actively embodied Christ's compassionate presence within his community. He addressed societal wrongs not merely as political or social issues but fundamentally as spiritual and theological matters—recognizing that Christ's incarnation called believers to stand in solidarity with the marginalized and oppressed.

---

[2] For additional studies on Francis James Grimké's life, ministry, and doctrinal convictions, see Eric J. Freeman, *Grimké's Gospel Echo: A Handbook for Preaching* (Columbia, SC: The Freeman Institute for Integrative Research, 2025), and Eric J. Freeman, "Pauline Echoes in the Preaching and Activism of Francis James Grimké (1850–1937): Confronting Ethnic Prejudice through an Evangelical Emancipatory Homiletic" (PhD diss., Anderson University, 2024), available on ProQuest.

His belief in the New Creation doctrine also significantly shaped his pastoral approach. Grimké emphasized that true transformation through Christ was available for individuals and communities alike. He tirelessly preached the power of redemption and renewal, urging his congregation and broader society to embody the new life made possible through Christ. His unwavering conviction in the transformative power of the gospel inspired enduring change, reconciliation, and hope within his community and beyond.

Contemporary Examples from Different Cultural Contexts

In rural Guatemala, a woman named Isabella struggled with syncretism—the blending of traditional Mayan religious practices with Christianity. After studying the doctrine of God's Triune Nature, she gained clarity about God's relational character. This understanding transformed how she approached her community relationships, leading her to start a reconciliation ministry between divided family clans in her village. Her clear grasp of God's unity-in-diversity provided a theological foundation for her peacemaking work.

In South Korea, Pastor Kim applied the doctrine of Eschatology to address the high-pressure academic culture affecting many youth in his congregation. By teaching the ultimate hope of God's renewed creation, he helped students develop a balanced perspective that valued academic excellence while rejecting society's idolization of achievement. This resulted in a youth ministry characterized by both academic support and genuine spiritual formation, rather than competition.

In an Australian urban context, a business leader named James found that the doctrine of Original Sin gave him a framework for implementing more compassionate corporate policies. Recognizing human fallibility, including his own, led him to create workplace structures that promoted accountability with grace, changing his company's culture from fear-based performance to trust-based collaboration.

These examples from diverse cultural settings illustrate how sound doctrine transcends geographical boundaries while addressing contextually specific challenges, demonstrating the universal yet culturally adaptable nature of biblical truth.

The Social Implications of Sound Doctrine

Sound doctrine and social ethics are intrinsically connected and together form the heartbeat of the gospel. Doctrine provides the predicates—the foundational truths about God, humanity, and redemption—that shape our understanding of who God is and what He has done. These truths, in turn, inform the indicatives—how we are to live and act in response to God's transformative work in Christ.

For instance, the doctrine of Incarnation teaches us about God's compassionate entry into human suffering, compelling us as believers to reflect this same compassion by actively engaging with those experiencing injustice, oppression, and hardship.

Similarly, a clear understanding of Original Sin helps us recognize systemic and individual brokenness, driving us toward humility, repentance, and practical efforts at reconciliation and restoration within our communities.

The doctrine of the New Creation reminds us that Christ's redemptive work is holistic, affecting not only individual souls but also societal structures and relationships. This truth motivates believers to embody transformative actions such as forgiveness, peacebuilding, and community restoration. Likewise, a robust grasp of Eschatology provides a hopeful vision for the future, empowering Christians to courageously address present injustices, knowing that our work for justice and mercy anticipates and participates in God's ultimate renewal of all things.

Contemporary Application: Doctrine and Modern Challenges

Today's believers face distinctive challenges that sound doctrine helps address:

- **Digital Ethics**: The doctrine of Canon (Scripture) provides timeless principles for navigating internet use, digital honesty, and online relationships.
- **Environmental Stewardship**: Understanding Creation and Eschatology informs how we care for the earth as both God's present creation and the precursor to the renewed creation.
- **Racial Reconciliation**: Doctrines of Original Sin, Incarnation, and New Creation offer profound resources

for addressing historical injustices and pursuing meaningful unity.

- **Mental Health**: The doctrine of God's Triune Nature reveals a God who understands relationship, suffering, and healing, informing compassionate approaches to mental health challenges.

Ultimately, doctrine and social ethics are inseparable aspects of genuine gospel living. Sound doctrine is not merely intellectual affirmation; it compels active, transformative engagement in society, guiding believers to embody Christ's love, justice, and mercy in practical and tangible ways.

Practical Application Exercise: Doctrinal Integration

Choose one area of your life where you face regular challenges (work, family relationships, personal spiritual growth, community involvement, etc.). Select two doctrines from the D.O.C.T.R.I.N.E. framework that seem most relevant to this area. Use the following steps to integrate these doctrines into your daily practice:

1. **Identify**: Name the specific challenges you face in this area of life.

2. **Connect**: Write down how each doctrine specifically addresses these challenges.

3. **Envision**: Describe what living according to these doctrinal truths would look like practically.

4. **Implement**: Create 2-3 concrete action steps based on these doctrines.

5. **Share**: Find a trusted friend with whom you can discuss your insights and who will hold you accountable for your action steps.

6. **Reflect**: After one week, evaluate how your doctrinal understanding has shaped your actions and attitudes.

This exercise helps move doctrine from abstract knowledge to lived experience, demonstrating the power of theological truth for everyday transformation.

Reflection Questions

1. Reflect on your experiences or observations: Why do you think some Christians perceive doctrine as impractical or overly academic? How can this perception be positively changed?

2. How does understanding these eight core doctrinal truths influence your personal choices, priorities, and relationships in daily life?

3. In what specific ways can you practically embody and demonstrate sound doctrine within your family, church, workplace, or broader community?

4. Which doctrinal area discussed in this chapter challenges you the most? Why? What steps will you take to deepen your understanding and apply this truth in your daily life?

5. Consider a pressing social issue in your community or nation. How might one or more of these doctrines provide wisdom and guidance for Christians seeking to engage this issue redemptively?

6. How can your clearer understanding of doctrine help you better communicate and live out the gospel with authenticity, clarity, and compassion?

Conclusion: From Knowledge to Transformation

As we conclude this introductory exploration of doctrine, it becomes clear that doctrine encompasses much more than a collection of intellectual beliefs—it embodies the vibrant truth of God meant to shape every aspect of our lives. When properly understood, doctrine not only strengthens our personal faith but also encourages us to engage actively in God's redemptive work in the world.

With this foundational understanding, we are now ready to delve deeper into each specific doctrine, starting with the essential truth of Christ's Deity. Understanding who Jesus truly is will profoundly influence how we relate to Him, worship Him, and represent Him in our daily interactions. As we turn the page, let us prepare our hearts and minds to encounter Christ anew—fully God, fully deserving of our devotion, and deeply present in every moment of our lives.

Looking Ahead: The Deity of Christ

The next chapter will explore the foundational doctrine of Christ's deity—the "D" in our D.O.C.T.R.I.N.E. framework. We'll examine biblical evidence for Christ's divine nature, address common misconceptions, and discover how recognizing Jesus as fully God transforms our worship, witness, and daily walk. This doctrine isn't merely theological; it's the bedrock for understanding the gospel itself and experiencing the full power of Christ's presence in our lives.

1

Deity

Jesus is God: Knowing Who He Really Is

✛

In the beginning was the Word, and the Word was with God, and the Word was God. He was in the beginning with God. All things were made through him, and without him was not any thing made that was made.

John 1:1--3 (ESV)

At the core of the Christian faith is the foundational truth that Jesus Christ is fully God, the eternal and divine Word of God. Recognizing Jesus as God is essential because it defines His authority, His capacity for redemption, and His rightful worship as God alone.

Biblical Affirmation of Christ's Deity

The Bible clearly affirms Christ's deity throughout both the Old and New Testaments. In the Old Testament, Isaiah prophesied about the coming Messiah, declaring, "For to us a child is born, to us a son is given... and his name shall be called Wonderful Counselor, Mighty God, Everlasting Father, Prince of Peace" (Isaiah 9:6), directly attributing divine titles to the promised deliverer.

In the New Testament, John 1:1-14 identifies Jesus as the eternal Word (Logos) who was not only present with God at creation but is God Himself, the source and creator of all things. Similarly, in John 10:30, Jesus explicitly declares, "I and the Father are one," directly affirming His divine unity and equality with God. Colossians 1:15-20 describes Jesus as the "image of the invisible God," underscoring His divine nature and role as the creator and sustainer of the universe.

Clarifying Reflection: A practical illustration of understanding God's nature is found in the opening chapters of Genesis and the Gospel of John. Genesis reveals God as the creator who speaks creation into existence—His Word holding the power to create and sustain life. In John's Gospel, Jesus is revealed explicitly as this creative Word, confirming His role as the active agent in creation and thus affirming His full deity.

Historical Affirmation of Christ's Deity

This understanding has been historically affirmed by the church across diverse cultures and traditions. The Council of Nicaea (AD 325) stood firmly against the Arian controversy, which erroneously argued that Jesus was a created being. The council emphatically asserted the eternal deity of Christ, articulated through the Nicene Creed, which declares Jesus Christ to be "God from God, Light from Light, true God from true God." This affirmation remains a bedrock of Christian orthodoxy, establishing the crucial recognition of Jesus' divine nature.

In simple terms, recognizing Jesus as God means understanding that He is not just a great teacher or prophet, but truly God Himself, sharing the same nature, authority, and power as God the Father. This truth shapes our faith, guides our worship, and assures us that Jesus has the power and right to transform our lives and the world.

Why His Deity Matters for Everyday Life

Recognizing the deity of Christ powerfully impacts our everyday lives, providing believers with assurance, guidance, and purpose. Jesus, as fully God, holds authority over all creation, affirming His promises and His capacity to fulfill them. Colossians 1:16-17 reminds us, "For by him all things were created, in heaven and on earth, visible and invisible... And he is before all things, and in him all things hold together." Because He is God, His teachings are not merely moral suggestions but divine truths essential to discipleship.

Christ was not just a great teacher, prophet, or healer. He was more than these things. While a teacher can fix ignorance, and a healer can mend physical ailments, only God can open our spiritual eyes and redeem our souls from sin's eternal consequences. This profound truth elevates the significance of Christ's identity and mission.

Real-Life Application: Consider Maria, a community organizer in an under-resourced neighborhood facing systemic challenges. When crisis struck her community following a natural disaster, her understanding of Jesus' deity transformed her approach. Rather than seeing herself as carrying the burden alone, she recognized that the God who created all things was working through her efforts. This perspective gave her both peace in uncertainty and confidence to persevere when resources seemed scarce. Her prayers shifted from desperation to expectation, knowing that Christ's divine power and authority were greater than the challenges her community faced.

Practically, embracing Christ's divine nature means trusting His sovereign control during uncertainty, drawing upon His strength amidst personal and collective challenges, and seeking clarity from His divine wisdom in decision-making. In every aspect of daily life, acknowledging Christ's deity helps us to align our actions and attitudes with His divine authority and purpose, empowering us to live faithfully and impactfully.

Clarifying Reflection: When we truly grasp that Jesus is God, we approach prayer differently—not as wishful thinking, but as communion with the One who holds all power. We face challenges differently—not as victims of circumstance, but as people empowered by divine resources. We pursue justice differently—not merely as social activism, but as participation in God's redemptive work in the world.

Common Misconceptions About His Deity

Despite the clear biblical affirmation, misconceptions about Christ's deity often arise across various cultural and religious contexts.

One common misunderstanding is that Jesus was merely a divine messenger or prophet, lacking full divine essence. This view, common in some world religions and even certain Christianadjacent movements, diminishes Jesus' nature and role. Scripture corrects this by repeatedly affirming Jesus' equality and unity with God the Father (John 10:30, Philippians 2:6).

Another frequent confusion is the idea that Jesus' deity diminishes His humanity. The truth is, biblical teaching robustly affirms both His full deity and full humanity simultaneously (Hebrews 4:15). Recognizing this dual nature is critical to understanding Christ's unique capacity to redeem humanity fully. In other words, because Jesus is both fully human and fully divine, He uniquely bridges the gap between humanity and God, making Him perfectly capable of fully restoring our relationship with God.

Some contemporary skeptics argue that Jesus' deity was a later invention of the church, not present in early Christian teachings. Yet historical scholarship demonstrates that early Christian worship, writings, and practices all reflected a belief in Jesus' divine nature. The earliest Christian hymns and confessions, some preserved in the New Testament itself (Philippians 2:5-11, Colossians 1:15-20), clearly express belief in Christ's deity.

Lastly, some argue Jesus never explicitly claimed to be God. Yet, Jesus made clear statements equating Himself with God, accepted worship reserved only for God, and demonstrated divine authority by forgiving sins and performing miracles. Understanding these realities helps clarify misconceptions, strengthening our faith in His deity.

Clarifying Reflection: These misconceptions matter because an incomplete view of Jesus leads to an incomplete experience of salvation. If Jesus is merely a prophet or teacher, His death could not atone for our sins. If He is God but not truly human, He could not represent us. The biblical Jesus—fully God and fully human—is uniquely qualified to be our Savior.

How to Communicate Christ's Deity to Others

Communicating the deity of Christ effectively begins with a clear, simple explanation grounded in Scripture. Using key passages such as John 1:1-14, John 10:30, and Colossians 1:15-20 can clearly establish biblical support.

When engaging with people from different faith backgrounds, approach the conversation with both confidence in truth and respect for the person. Listen carefully to understand their perspective before responding. For someone from a Muslim background, for instance, you might acknowledge their high view of Jesus as a prophet while gently exploring what Jesus himself claimed about His identity. With someone from a secular background, starting with Jesus' moral teachings and then exploring what authority would be needed to make such claims might be effective.

Practical tips for sharing include:

- Emphasizing the relevance of Christ's deity to personal redemption
- Offering personal testimony of its impact in your life

- Addressing common questions or objections gently yet confidently

- Using analogies that make complex theological concepts accessible

- Being patient, recognizing that understanding often develops gradually

Cultural bridges can also help. In communities where ancestral wisdom is highly valued, explaining how Jesus fulfills and exceeds the hopes of our ancestors can resonate deeply. In contexts where justice issues are paramount, emphasizing how Christ's deity empowers lasting transformation can provide meaningful connection.

Most importantly, demonstrating Christ's deity through transformed character and authentic Christian living powerfully reinforces the spoken message, providing credibility and tangible evidence of its transformative truth. As Dr. Howard Thurman observed, people are more convinced by lives that embody truth than by arguments alone.

Clarifying Reflection: Effective communication about Christ's deity isn't about winning theological arguments but about inviting others to encounter the living God in the person of Jesus Christ. Our goal is not merely intellectual agreement but life transformation through relationship with Him.

Deity and Worship

Understanding Jesus as fully God significantly shapes how we worship. Recognizing Christ's divine nature calls believers to worship Him with reverence, awe, and adoration, acknowledging His majesty, holiness, and sovereign power.

Scripture models this reverential worship, exemplified when Thomas, upon recognizing Jesus' deity, proclaimed, "My Lord and my God!" (John 20:28). Likewise, Revelation presents a vivid picture of Christ receiving worship in heavenly realms, affirming His deity and rightful place at the center of Christian worship (Revelation 5:12-13).

This theological understanding finds expression in worship practices across various traditions. In many African American churches, for example, the call-and-response pattern reflects a dynamic interaction with the living Christ. Hymns like "Jesus, the Light of the World" celebrate His divine nature through both lyrics and the embodied experience of congregational singing. Similarly, worship songs like "Total Praise" by Richard Smallwood express complete surrender to Christ's divine lordship.

Worship practices that particularly honor Christ's deity include:

- Communion/Eucharist, which commemorates His divine sacrifice
- Corporate confession, which acknowledges His divine authority to forgive

- Responsive readings of Scripture that declare His divine attributes

- Moments of contemplative silence that create space to experience His divine presence

Practically, worshipping Jesus as God encourages a deeper personal devotion and informs corporate worship practices, fostering a community united in adoration of Christ. Embracing His deity elevates our worship beyond mere rituals, transforming it into genuine encounters with the living God.

Clarifying Reflection: When we truly worship Jesus as God, our worship becomes not just an expression of religious obligation but a transformative encounter that renews our minds, heals our hearts, and empowers our witness in the world.

Supplemental Materials

Recommended Reading:

- "The Case for Christ" by Lee Strobel for an investigative approach to understanding and affirming Jesus' deity

- "God Is Not Black, God Is Not White" by Reggie White for a culturally relevant exploration of Christ's divine nature

- "Jesus and the Disinherited" by Howard Thurman for insights on how Christ's deity empowers marginalized communities

Practical Exercises:

- Meditate daily on key scriptures affirming Christ's deity (John 1, Colossians 1, Hebrews 1)

- Reflect in a journal how this shapes your view of Christ and daily decisions

- Practice explaining Christ's deity in simple terms to different hypothetical audiences

- Create a personal worship experience focusing specifically on Christ's divine attributes

Suggested Resources:

- Listen to sermons or teachings from influential African American preachers such as Gardner C. Taylor, E.V. Hill, Tony Evans, or Robert Smith, whose ministries deeply emphasize the deity of Christ and its transformative power

- Explore worship music from diverse cultural traditions that celebrate Christ's deity

- Study artwork depicting Christ from various cultural perspectives to broaden your appreciation of His universal divine nature

Reflection Questions

1. What does believing in Christ's divinity change about your daily decisions?

2. How might fully embracing Jesus as God reshape your response to personal struggles or societal injustices?

3. Can you think of a specific area in your life where acknowledging Christ's deity might alter your approach or attitude?

4. How has your cultural background influenced your understanding of Christ's divine nature?

5. In what ways does recognizing Jesus as God impact how you relate to authorities in your life?

Final Thoughts & Next Steps

Understanding the deity of Christ lays a solid foundation for every believer's faith journey. As we grasp the significance of Jesus as fully God, we begin to experience deeper faith, clearer purpose, and greater spiritual transformation. This truth transcends cultural boundaries, offering hope and empowerment to believers across diverse communities and contexts.

The recognition of Jesus' deity isn't merely an intellectual exercise but an invitation to experience the living God in a personal, transformative relationship. Allow this profound truth to continually shape your heart, mind, and actions as you navigate both personal challenges and community engagement.

In the next chapter, we will explore the doctrine of Original Sin, uncovering why recognizing our fallen state is critical to appreciating the full depth and power of Christ's redemptive work.

2

Original Sin

Born Broken, Redeemed Whole

✦

In the beginning was the Word, and the Word was with God, and the Word was God. He was in the beginning with God. All things were made through him, and without him was not any thing made that was made.

John 1:1--3 (ESV)

What is Original Sin, and Why Does It Matter?

A t the heart of the Christian faith is an honest recognition of our human condition. Original sin describes the fundamental truth that humanity enters this world already marked by sinfulness, a nature inherently broken and inclined toward rebellion against God. As Psalm 51:5 poignantly captures, "Surely I was sinful at birth, sinful from the time my mother conceived me." We are born into a predicament—not simply a problem to solve, but an identity crisis: we are fundamentally disconnected from God's original intent for humanity.

Original sin is more than personal failures or moral slip-ups; it represents a deeper condition of spiritual brokenness and estrangement from God. As Apostle Paul clarifies, "all have sinned and fall short of the glory of God" (Romans 3:23). Recognizing original sin is crucial because without understanding our true condition, the redemptive story of Jesus Christ loses its significance. Christ did not merely come to improve good people;

He came because humanity was utterly incapable of self-rescue. If we deny the depth of our sinfulness, we inadvertently diminish the purpose and necessity of Christ's sacrifice (Galatians 2:21).

Yet, the story doesn't end in despair. It begins there. By honestly facing our brokenness, we can genuinely embrace the transformative power of God's redemption through Christ.

Original Blessing and Identity

Before humanity's fall into sin, we were created in the image of God, reflecting His dignity, beauty, and purpose. This original blessing defines our true identity. Psalm 139:14 describes us as "fearfully and wonderfully made," underscoring our intrinsic worth and intentional design by God. God created humanity not merely to exist, but to flourish, reflecting His character and stewarding creation as partners in His divine plan. This intended harmony between humanity and God is foundational to understanding our worth and purpose.

This foundational blessing means that every person, despite the presence of sin, retains intrinsic dignity and value. Sin does not erase our fundamental worth; instead, it obscures and distorts our self-perception and relationship with God. The distortion created by sin convinces us to define ourselves by our mistakes, failures, or brokenness rather than by our created purpose and divine origin. Our journey toward redemption, therefore, involves rediscovering and reclaiming this foundational blessing as our core identity.

When we fully appreciate the magnitude of our original blessing, we are empowered to embrace our redemption with greater hope and clarity. Redemption is not just about reversing the effects of sin; it is about restoring us to our original, divinely intended state of flourishing and wholeness. Recognizing our original blessing enables us to approach God and others with humility, compassion, and profound gratitude, understanding that our identity is deeply rooted in God's original intent and unchanging love.

Sin as Separation from God's Original Intent

Sin, at its core, is anything that separates us from God and His original intent for humanity. It is not merely a list of moral infractions; it is fundamentally a rupture in our relationship with our Creator. Isaiah 59:2 says, "Your iniquities have separated you from your God." This separation leads to spiritual death and a perpetual struggle with identity and purpose. Recognizing sin as relational rather than simply legalistic helps us understand why Christ's mission involved not just sacrifice but reconciliation.

The relational nature of sin also affects our interactions with one another and the world around us. Our broken relationship with God manifests in broken relationships with others—marked by conflict, misunderstanding, and injustice. Sin distorts not only our perception of self but also how we view and treat others, creating societal fractures and injustices. The ripple effects of sin's relational disruption extend into every aspect of human experience, underscoring our desperate need for restoration.

Furthermore, sin is not just an individual issue; it is systemic and pervasive. It influences institutions, cultures, and systems, embedding patterns of injustice, oppression, and inequality into societal structures. This systemic dimension manifests in concrete ways: economic systems that prioritize profit over human dignity, racial prejudices that become institutionalized in laws and practices, environmental exploitation that disregards our stewardship responsibility, and religious structures that can promote exclusion rather than God's inclusive love. For example, the wealth gap between rich and poor reflects not merely individual choices but systemic patterns that perpetuate inequality contrary to God's desire for human flourishing and justice (Micah 6:8). Similarly, historical patterns of discrimination become embedded in cultural assumptions and institutional policies, creating barriers that extend far beyond individual prejudices.

Recognizing these systemic manifestations of sin challenges Christians to address not only personal sinfulness but also the broader implications of sin in society. True reconciliation involves repairing these ruptures on every level—personal, relational, and societal. As followers of Christ, we are called to confront these systems with prophetic courage while modeling alternatives that reflect God's kingdom values of justice, compassion, and human dignity.

Original Sin and the Necessity of Redemption

Given the pervasive and profound nature of original sin, it becomes evident why redemption through Christ is not just beneficial but absolutely essential. Humanity, left to its own devices, remains trapped in a cycle of brokenness and spiritual death. Romans 5:19 articulates clearly, "For just as through the disobedience of the one man the many were made sinners, so also through the obedience of the one man the many will be made righteous." Only through divine intervention could the catastrophic consequences of humanity's fall be adequately addressed. The severity of original sin demands a Savior capable of bridging the infinite chasm between fallen humanity and a holy God.

Christ's incarnation—God taking on flesh and dwelling among us—is central to understanding redemption. By fully embodying human nature, Jesus entered into our broken reality, confronting and ultimately defeating sin's power through His life, death, and resurrection. The incarnation makes redemption profoundly personal; it demonstrates God's unwavering commitment to reconcile us back to Himself, reaffirming our intrinsic value despite our sinfulness. Christ's mission was one of restoration, emphasizing that redemption isn't merely about escaping punishment but restoring our original created purpose and dignity.

Thus, redemption through Christ is transformative, changing our very nature and position before God. Galatians 2:21 underscores this necessity, stating, "If righteousness could be gained through the law, Christ died for nothing!" This powerful declaration emphasizes that no human effort, morality, or adherence to religious rules can overcome the effects of original sin. Redemption through Christ uniquely addresses the depth and breadth of our brokenness, bringing reconciliation not only with God but also restoring our identity and purpose. Understanding the necessity of redemption sets the stage for comprehending how Christ restores the image of God within us.

Restoring the Image of God Within Us

The doctrine of original sin is not an indictment meant to condemn, but a truthful diagnosis meant to lead us toward healing. It clarifies why humanity needs a Savior—someone capable of restoring our original identity as image-bearers of God.

Humanity was created in God's image—fearfully and wonderfully made (Psalm 139:14)—reflecting His nature, dignity, and goodness. Sin distorted this image, twisting our inclinations, and alienating us from our true selves and from God's original purpose. This distortion manifests not only in acts like lying or stealing, which we instinctively display even as children without being taught, but also in a profound internal disorientation: an identity crisis that convinces us we are something less than God's intended creation.

Jesus Christ, the second Adam, reverses this distortion (Romans 5:19). Through His sinless life, sacrificial death, and victorious resurrection, Christ redeems humanity, restoring the fractured image of God within us. His work reconciles justice and mercy—bearing the penalty for our sin while simultaneously renewing our relationship with God and reclaiming our true identity. Christ's redemption is not merely about forgiving past mistakes; it is fundamentally about restoring us to wholeness, aligning us once again with God's original blessing.

This restoration manifests in several concrete ways. First, we experience renewed communion with God, regaining the intimate relationship that was lost in Eden. Second, our perception changes as we begin to see ourselves through the lens of God's love rather than through the distorted lens of shame. Third, our desires and affections are gradually reordered, increasingly aligned with God's will as the Holy Spirit works within us. Fourth, we experience a new capacity for authentic community, as barriers between people begin to crumble in light of our shared redemption.

The process of restoration is both immediate and progressive. While our position before God changes instantly at the moment of salvation (justification), the working out of this reality in our daily lives (sanctification) unfolds throughout our lifetime. As 2 Corinthians 3:18 describes, "And we all, who with unveiled faces contemplate the Lord's glory, are being transformed into his image with ever-increasing glory, which comes from the Lord, who is the

Spirit." This transformation is not simply about moral improvement but about becoming more fully human as God originally intended—bearing His image with increasing clarity in a broken world.

Practical Implications: Living Redeemed

The reality of original sin and redemption has profound implications for daily Christian discipleship. Being redeemed means we live as new creations, fundamentally transformed and continuously shaped into Christ's image (2 Corinthians 5:17). This transformation involves not merely abstaining from sin but actively pursuing spiritual maturity and Christlikeness.

Philippians 3:13-14 urges believers to forget what is behind and strive toward what is ahead—living intentionally, empowered by the resurrection, to become who God always intended us to be. Living redeemed compels us to demonstrate grace, humility, and active compassion in our interactions with others, reflecting the transformative power of Christ's redemption in tangible, practical ways.

Living redeemed also means participating in God's work of restoration in the broader world. As those who have experienced redemption, we become agents of reconciliation (2 Corinthians 5:18-20), working to address both personal and systemic manifestations of sin. This might involve advocating for justice in public policy, creating economic opportunities for marginalized communities, practicing environmental stewardship, or fostering genuine racial reconciliation within our churches and communities. Our participation in these efforts is not merely social activism but an expression of our redeemed identity and a testimony to Christ's comprehensive work of restoration.

Ultimately, living redeemed means embracing our identity as God's beloved children and ambassadors of His kingdom. It means approaching each day with the humble recognition of our dependence on grace and the confident assurance that God is completing the good work He began in us (Philippians 1:6). In this tension between humility and confidence, we find the freedom to live authentically, love generously, and participate joyfully in God's ongoing work of redemption.

Reflection Questions

1. How does recognizing original sin influence your view of yourself and your dependence on Christ's grace?

2. In what ways has acknowledging your own spiritual brokenness made you more compassionate toward others?

3. What practical steps can you take this week to embrace the restored image of God within you, living authentically as a redeemed child of God?

4. How might you address systemic manifestations of sin in your community? Identify one area (economic inequality, racial injustice, environmental degradation, etc.) where you could begin to apply redemptive principles beyond just personal transformation.

5. In what ways does your understanding of being "restored in God's image" shape your daily decisions, relationships, and priorities? Where do you see evidence of this restoration already happening in your life?

3

Canon (Scripture)

Trusting the Story, the Reliability of God's Word

✝

All Scripture is God-breathed and is useful for teaching, rebuking, correcting and training in righteousness, so that the servant of God may be thoroughly equipped for every good work.

2 Timothy 3:16—17 (NIV)

Throughout history, people have sought to understand God's voice and will. The Bible stands as the primary means through which God has revealed Himself to humanity. This chapter explores the nature of scripture as the canon—the authoritative collection of sacred writings that forms the foundation of Christian faith and practice. We'll examine what makes scripture unique, how it came to be, why we can trust it, and how it transforms our daily lives, prayer, and communities.

What is the Canon?

The "Canon" refers to the Bible as the authoritative collection of sacred writings. The word "canon" itself means "measuring rod" or "standard," symbolizing how scripture functions as the standard for faith and practice. Christians believe these writings are inspired by the Holy Spirit and contain divine authority that guides believers in understanding God and His will for humanity (2 Timothy 3:16).

The Bible is divided into two major sections—the Old Testament and the New Testament. The Old Testament highlights humanity's need for God, showing the cycle of sin and the persistent inability of people to redeem themselves. The New Testament, on the other hand, demonstrates how God meets humanity's need through Jesus Christ, fulfilling the redemptive promise and establishing a new covenant (Hebrews 8:6-13).

This understanding of the canon shapes a believer's worldview, influencing personal choices, communal interactions, and broader social engagement.

CANON QUICK FACTS

Old Testament: 39 books (Protestant canon)

New Testament: 27 books

Written over: Approximately 1,500 years

Authors: More than 40 different writers

The Historical Formation of the Canon

The canon did not appear suddenly but developed through a careful process of recognition and affirmation. The Old Testament canon was largely established by the time of Jesus, who referred to "the Law of Moses, the Prophets and the Psalms" (Luke 24:44), acknowledging the three-part division of Hebrew scriptures.

For the New Testament, the early church applied several criteria to recognize which writings were divinely inspired:

1. **Apostolic Authority:** Was the book written by an apostle or someone closely associated with them?

2. **Universal Recognition**: Was the book widely accepted by churches across different regions?

3. **Consistent Message**: Did the content align with already accepted scripture and apostolic teaching?

4. **Spiritual Impact**: Did the writing demonstrate spiritual power to transform lives?

By the 4th century, the 27 books of our current New Testament were formally recognized, though most had been accepted much earlier. This process wasn't the church arbitrarily choosing books but rather recognizing what God had already inspired.

Different Canons in Christian Traditions

While Protestants recognize 66 books (39 Old Testament, 27 New Testament), Catholic and Orthodox traditions include additional books known as the Deuterocanonical works or Apocrypha. Catholics recognize 73 books, while Eastern Orthodox churches recognize up to 81 books. These differences emerged during the Reformation period over questions of original language, authorship, and consistency with other canonical writings.

Scripture as God's Revelation

Scripture is God's primary means of revealing Himself to humanity. From the very first words, "In the beginning..." (Genesis 1:1, John 1:1), the biblical narrative introduces God as Creator and initiator of relationship with humanity. Through stories, laws, poetry, prophecies, and letters, scripture conveys divine truths, guiding believers to know God personally and live in relationship with Him.

The Canon reveals God's character—His love, justice, mercy, and holiness. Reading scripture is not merely about acquiring knowledge but about encountering God Himself. It is through this divine encounter that believers grow spiritually and deepen their trust in God's promises and purposes (Hebrews 4:12).

Engaging scripture regularly transforms lives by renewing minds and shaping hearts, thus equipping believers for every good work (Romans 12:2).

Authority and Inspiration of Scripture

The authority of scripture rests in its divine inspiration—God breathing His message through human writers. This inspiration means that although human hands penned the words, the Holy Spirit guided the entire process, ensuring accuracy in conveying God's truths (2 Peter 1:20-21).

Because scripture is divinely inspired, it stands above tradition, reason, and experience as the ultimate measure of truth. Believers submit to its teachings, aligning their lives with its guidance, which shapes their moral and ethical behaviors.

Recognizing the divine origin of scripture instills confidence in believers, providing clarity and conviction to navigate life's complexities with biblical wisdom.

The Reliability and Trustworthiness of Scripture

Historical reliability and textual consistency affirm the trustworthiness of the Bible. Archeological findings, manuscript evidence, and fulfilled prophecies provide compelling support for the authenticity and preservation of biblical texts.

Archaeological Confirmations: Numerous archaeological discoveries have verified biblical accounts. For example, the Pool of Siloam mentioned in John 9 was discovered in Jerusalem in 2004, confirming the biblical description. The existence of King David, once questioned by critics, was confirmed by the Tel Dan Stele discovered in 1993, which mentions the "House of David."

Manuscript Evidence: With over 5,800 Greek New Testament manuscripts and fragments—some dating to within decades of the original writings—the Bible is the best-attested document from antiquity. The Dead Sea Scrolls, discovered in 1947, contained Old Testament texts dating from 250-100 BC, proving remarkable consistency with medieval manuscripts used for modern translations.

Textual Transmission: Ancient scribes developed sophisticated systems to ensure accurate copying of manuscripts, including counting letters and words. Even with minor variations in manuscripts, no core teaching of Christianity is affected by these variants.

Though composed over centuries by diverse authors from various cultures, scripture maintains a unified, coherent message centered around God's redemptive plan through Jesus Christ. This consistency further underscores its supernatural origin and reliability (Psalm 119:160).

The trustworthiness of scripture means believers can stake their lives and eternal destinies on its promises, shaping their worldview and daily living.

Common Questions About the Canon

Why weren't other ancient religious texts included in the Bible? Many writings were rejected because they appeared much later than the apostolic period, contained teachings contradictory to established scripture, lacked evidence of divine inspiration, or falsely claimed apostolic authorship. The Gnostic gospels, for example, were written in the 2nd-3rd centuries, long after the apostolic era, and presented views of Jesus inconsistent with earlier apostolic testimony.

Did church councils "create" the canon? Church councils formally recognized the canon but did not create it. They acknowledged books that had already demonstrated divine inspiration and had been widely used by believers. The Council of Hippo (393 AD) and Council of Carthage (397 AD) merely formalized what was already the practice of most churches.

How should we understand difficult or controversial passages? Scripture should be interpreted in light of its historical and literary context, the original audience, and the overall message of the Bible. Difficult passages should be understood in relation to clearer passages on the same topic. Remember that ancient texts reflected their cultural context while still conveying timeless truth.

The Practical Power of Praying Scripture

Praying scripture aligns believers with God's will and transforms prayer life. Using biblical texts in prayer, such as the Lord's Prayer (Matthew 6:9-13), helps believers to structure their communication with God effectively. The model of adoration, confession, thanksgiving, and supplication (ACTS) finds its roots in scriptural examples and provides practical guidance for personal and corporate prayer.

A Simple Framework for Scripture Prayer:

1. **Read**: Select a passage that speaks to your situation or need

2. **Reflect**: Consider what the passage reveals about God or His will

3. **Respond**: Turn the passage into a personal prayer

4. **Rest**: Quietly listen for God's response

Example: Reading Psalm 23:1 ("The Lord is my shepherd; I shall not want"), you might pray: "Lord, I acknowledge you as my shepherd today. Thank you for your promise to provide for my needs. Help me trust you with my current financial concerns. I surrender my anxiety about _____ and choose to rest in your care."

Integrating scripture into prayer deepens intimacy with God and empowers believers to pray confidently, knowing they echo

God's own words. It enhances personal devotion and enriches corporate worship experiences.

Scripture-centered prayer strengthens believers spiritually, equips them to overcome life's challenges, and aligns their hearts with God's purposes.

Living the Scripture Daily

Scripture's transformative power extends beyond knowledge acquisition, urging practical application in everyday life. Believers are encouraged to internalize and practice biblical teachings, thereby manifesting Christ-like behaviors and attitudes (James 1:22).

Practical Tools for Scripture Engagement:

1. **Meditation Framework**: (The "SOAP" Method)

   - **S**cripture: Read a passage slowly

   - **O**bservation: Note what stands out to you

   - **A**pplication: Identify how it applies to your life

   - **P**rayer: Respond to God about what you've learned

2. **Memorization Techniques**:

   - Write verses on index cards for review

   - Set scripture to music

   - Use memory apps like "Bible Memory"

   - Practice with a partner for accountability

3. **Application in Specific Situations**:

   - **Work decisions**: Colossians 3:23 guides work ethic

- **Family conflict**: Ephesians 4:29-32 shapes communication
- **Financial choices**: Proverbs 3:9-10 directs priorities
- **Anxiety management**: Philippians 4:6-7 offers a pathway to peace

Regular engagement with scripture cultivates character, promotes ethical living, and guides believers in making decisions that honor God and reflect His kingdom values.

Real-Life Example: When James faced an ethical dilemma at work—being asked to slightly misrepresent data on a report—he remembered Proverbs 11:1 ("The Lord detests dishonest scales, but accurate weights find favor with him"). This scripture gave him clarity and courage to respectfully decline and suggest an honest alternative, which his supervisor ultimately appreciated.

Scripture's Role in Community and Discipleship

The Bible functions powerfully in community life, shaping corporate worship, communal relationships, and collective mission. Scriptural teaching provides foundational guidance for churches, shaping their identity, unity, and mission-driven efforts.

In discipleship, scripture serves as the primary resource for spiritual growth, equipping believers to mentor others effectively. The community of believers is strengthened as they learn together, hold one another accountable, and apply biblical truths in mutual encouragement and collective action (Colossians 3:16).

Communal Scripture Practices:

- Lectio Divina: A group practice of reading, meditation, prayer, and contemplation
- Scripture-based small group discussions
- Memorizing passages together
- Collaborative service projects based on biblical mandates

Ultimately, scripture unifies the body of Christ, guiding collective actions toward justice, reconciliation, and gospel proclamation in a divided world, emphasizing that discipleship occurs most effectively within scripturally grounded communities.

Connection to Previous and Upcoming Chapters

In Chapter 2, we explored "Original Sin" and how we are born broken but redeemed whole. The Canon we've examined in this chapter provides the authoritative source for understanding both our fallen condition and God's redemptive plan. Scripture reliably reveals the reality of sin and the path to restoration, themes we explored previously.

Looking ahead to Chapter 4 on the "Triune Nature of God ('Trinity')," we'll see how scripture reveals God as Father, Son, and Holy Spirit. The reliability of scripture we've established here gives us confidence to trust these profound revelations about God's nature, even when they transcend full human comprehension. The Canon provides the foundation for our Trinitarian understanding and worship.

Reflection Questions

1. How can you practically incorporate more scripture into your daily routine? Which of the meditation or memorization methods might work best for you?

2. What specific Bible verses or passages have significantly influenced your spiritual growth? How have they shaped your understanding of God?

3. How does viewing scripture as divinely inspired change your approach to reading and applying it? Does this view create any challenges for you?

4. What role does praying scripture currently play in your prayer life, and how can you enhance it using the framework provided?

5. How can your community or small group better integrate scripture into collective discipleship and service? What practices might you suggest implementing?

6. Consider a current decision or challenge you face. Which biblical passages might provide guidance, and how would you apply them to your situation?

4

The Triune Nature of God ("Trinity")

God with Us: Father, Son, & Holy Spirit

✦

For there are three that bear witness in heaven: the Father, the Word,
and the Holy Spirit; and these three are one.

1 John 5:7 (NKJV)

Having explored the authority and reliability of Scripture in the previous chapter, we now turn to what that Scripture reveals about the very nature of God Himself. The doctrine of the Trinity expresses one of the most profound and mysterious truths of the Christian faith: there is one God, eternally existent in three distinct persons—Father, Son, and Holy Spirit. This teaching, while challenging to fully comprehend with our finite minds, invites us into deeper understanding of God's infinite nature.

Scripture introduces us to this reality from the very beginning. In Genesis 1, God speaks creation into existence through His Word, revealing the Father's role as the creator. The Spirit of God hovers over the waters, signifying His life-giving presence. Likewise, the Gospel of John affirms Jesus as the Word made flesh (John 1:14), illustrating the redemptive dimension of the Son's role. This understanding builds upon our exploration of Christ's deity in Chapter 1 and provides the foundation for understanding the resurrection we will explore in Chapter 5.

Each person of the Trinity embodies distinct roles, yet remains fully unified in divine essence. The Father is the source and creator, the Son is the redeemer, and the Spirit is the life-giver. Together, these roles reveal the manifold nature of God, each necessary to fully express the completeness of God's character and work in creation and redemption.

It's important to recognize that the Trinity is not a division of God into three separate deities—a misunderstanding that would contradict the Bible's clear teaching on monotheism. Rather, this doctrine affirms that the one true God exists in a unity of being with three distinct expressions or persons.

Practically, recognizing the Trinity helps believers appreciate the comprehensive nature of salvation: created by the Father, redeemed by the Son, and empowered by the Holy Spirit.

The Father: Source and Sustainer

God the Father is often associated with creation, provision, and sovereign rule. The term "Father" signifies God's role as the ultimate source and originator of all things. As believers, understanding God as Father deepens our intimacy with Him. He is not merely a distant creator but a loving parent who guides, disciplines, and nurtures.

This fatherhood is exemplified in scriptures such as James 1:17, where every good gift is attributed to the Father of lights. Believers are invited to trust in the Father's provision and care, recognizing His sovereignty and kindness. Embracing God as Father transforms our prayer life, empowering us to approach Him with confidence and intimacy, assured of His love and attention to our needs.

In daily discipleship, this knowledge shapes our identity, fostering security and belonging, knowing we are adopted into God's family (Romans 8:15). This adoption restores us to right relationship with our heavenly Father despite our inherent brokenness.

The Son: Redeemer and Mediator

God the Son, Jesus Christ, embodies redemption. Through His incarnation, life, death, and resurrection, He accomplished the ultimate act of salvation. Jesus became flesh, fully human yet fully God, enabling Him to mediate perfectly between humanity and God. He experienced human frailties without succumbing to sin, fulfilling righteousness on our behalf.

The significance of the Son is captured beautifully in John 1:14, highlighting Jesus as the living embodiment of grace and truth. Christ's dual nature as fully God and fully human means He can stand in our place, paying the penalty for sin while also demonstrating God's unwavering justice and mercy. This is illustrated in the Pauline concept of Jesus as the second Adam who redeems humanity from the first Adam's fall (1 Corinthians 15:21-22).

Understanding Christ's redeeming work transforms our daily lives by grounding our faith in His completed work, encouraging us to live from a position of grace, freedom, and gratitude. His victorious resurrection and divine-human nature continue to shape our identity and purpose as believers.

The Holy Spirit: Animator and Empowerer

The Holy Spirit, often called the Spirit of life, animates, empowers, and transforms believers. Genesis portrays the Spirit as life-giving, breathing life into humanity (Genesis 2:7). Likewise, in the New Testament, the Spirit is described as the Comforter, Advocate, and Helper sent by Christ (John 14:26).

The Spirit quickens believers spiritually, enabling them to live transformed lives. The work of the Spirit is evident in regeneration, sanctification, and empowerment for witness and service. By living in dependence on the Holy Spirit, believers can experience a life marked by spiritual fruit—love, joy, peace, patience, and more (Galatians 5:22-23).

Acknowledging the Spirit's role enhances personal holiness, energizes prayer and worship, and equips believers for effective ministry and witness in the world. Through the Spirit's ongoing work, we experience spiritual rebirth and transformation into Christ's image.

The Divine Dance: Unity and Distinction

Christian theologians have described the Trinity using the term "perichoresis," a divine choreography or harmonious relationship among the Father, Son, and Holy Spirit. This relationship is unified yet distinct, illustrating perfect cooperation and mutual indwelling without division or hierarchy. This concept emphasizes that the Trinity is not three separate gods but one God in three persons.

This unity is essential for understanding salvation history. Each person of the Trinity operates harmoniously—creating, redeeming, and sanctifying—in seamless cooperation. This divine unity models relational harmony for believers, informing how we interact within community and family, mirroring divine love and cooperation.

Embracing this divine unity and distinction helps believers appreciate diversity within unity, inspiring greater humility, cooperation, and love in personal relationships and church communities. This understanding shapes how we read Scripture and how we live in community as the body of Christ.

Avoiding Misunderstandings

Throughout history, various understandings about God's nature have emerged as believers sought to honor biblical teaching while emphasizing God's oneness. Some traditions express concern that Trinitarian concepts might seem to suggest multiple deities rather than one God. Others focus primarily on one aspect of God's nature, potentially overlooking the fullness of God's self-revelation in Scripture.

Different theological traditions affirm that God is one while acknowledging the biblical witness to the Father, Son, and Holy Spirit. This perspective aims to preserve monotheism while embracing the rich complexity of how God has revealed Himself throughout Scripture and salvation history.

Christians across various traditions share a commitment to honoring God's unity, even when they understand the biblical witness differently. In conversations with believers who emphasize different aspects of God's nature, we can find common ground in our shared commitment to monotheism while respectfully exploring how Scripture reveals God's character and work.

By approaching these conversations with humility and grace, believers can engage meaningfully with those who may understand this doctrine differently, promoting dialogue rather than division. Clear understanding of biblical teaching helps believers communicate effectively about their faith while promoting unity in essentials and charity in differences.

The Triune Nature in Worship and Prayer

Our understanding of God's triune nature profoundly shapes worship and prayer. When believers pray to the Father through the Son by the power of the Spirit, they engage with the fullness of God's being. This trinitarian pattern appears throughout Scripture and Christian tradition, enriching our devotional lives.

In worship, we celebrate each aspect of God's nature—praising the Father's creation and provision, the Son's redemption and teaching, and the Spirit's guidance and empowerment. Many traditional hymns and contemporary worship songs reflect this pattern, helping believers express adoration to God in His fullness.

Prayer becomes more vibrant when we recognize we can approach the Father with the same intimacy Jesus demonstrated, speak to Jesus as our present Lord and friend, and depend on the Spirit's help in our weakness. This comprehensive approach to prayer engages the complete biblical witness to God's nature and work.

Practically, this understanding encourages believers to develop a balanced spiritual life that honors all aspects of God's self-revelation, avoiding overemphasis on any single dimension that might limit our experience of God's complete character and work in our lives.

Reflection Questions

1. How does understanding the triune nature of God deepen your relationship with Him and enhance your reading of Scripture?

2. In what practical ways does recognizing God's triune nature influence your daily worship and prayer?

3. How can you communicate this doctrine to others, particularly those unfamiliar or who may have different understandings?

4. How might you graciously discuss God's nature with believers from different theological traditions, focusing on shared commitments to honor the one true God?

5. How does the Trinity help you understand your identity as someone created in God's image yet affected by original sin?

5

Resurrection

Life After Death, Hope Beyond the Grave

✝

*Jesus said to her, "I am the resurrection and the life. Whoever believes
in me, though he die, yet shall he live, and everyone who lives and
believes in me shall never die. Do you believe this?"*

John 11:25—26 (ESV)

The Historical Foundation of Resurrection

The resurrection of Jesus Christ stands at the heart of
Christian faith, offering a firm historical foundation upon
which believers stake their hope. Unlike mythological narratives,
the resurrection is anchored in verifiable historical evidence.
Roman soldiers, experts in execution, testified to His death, and
numerous historical documents affirm His bodily resurrection.
His tomb remains empty—a powerful testimony to His victory
over death.

Consider the case of Thomas, who declared he would not
believe unless he could place his fingers in Christ's wounds. When
the risen Jesus appeared before him, Thomas's skepticism
transformed into profound faith as he proclaimed, "My Lord and
my God!" (John 20:28). This encounter illustrates how the
resurrection confronted and overcame even the most determined
doubt.

Similarly, the apostle Paul, once a persecutor of Christians,
had his life radically transformed after encountering the risen

Christ on the Damascus road. His willingness to endure imprisonment, beatings, and eventually martyrdom testifies to the reality of what he witnessed.

Reflection: How does the historical evidence for the resurrection strengthen your confidence in the truth of the Christian faith? What would you say to someone who doubts the resurrection's historicity?

Resurrection as the Conquest of Sin, Death, and Evil

In conquering death, Jesus decisively addressed humanity's most profound enemy—sin and its ultimate consequence, death. The apostle Paul succinctly captured this truth, declaring that if Christ was not raised, our faith would be futile, and humanity would remain trapped in sin (1 Corinthians 15:17). Resurrection marks Christ's definitive victory over the dominion of evil, sin, and spiritual death.

This victory powerfully completes what was revealed about God's nature in the previous chapter. The Triune God—Father, Son, and Holy Spirit—works in perfect harmony to accomplish redemption. The Father sends the Son, the Son willingly offers Himself, and the Spirit raises Him to life (Romans 8:11). In the resurrection, we see the fullness of divine power expressing the perfect love within the Trinity.

Imagine standing at a graveside, confronting the finality of death. Now picture that grave suddenly empty, its occupant alive and transformed. That is precisely the stunning reversal that occurred at Christ's resurrection and what awaits all who trust in Him. Death—once the undefeatable enemy—has lost its sting. As C.S. Lewis famously noted, "Death is the great iconoclast," but through Christ's resurrection, death itself has been defeated.

Reflection: How does understanding the resurrection as victory over sin and death affect how you view your personal struggles with sin? What specific "death" in your life needs resurrection power today?

Living in the Resurrection's Transformative Power

Believers today are invited to experience the resurrection's power in practical, transformative ways. Resurrection power liberates believers not merely from sin's penalty but also progressively from its daily presence and power.

Maria, a recovering addict, describes her experience: "Before knowing Christ, I was spiritually dead, trapped in a cycle of substance abuse that destroyed my relationships and nearly took my life. But when I encountered Jesus, it was like being raised from death to life. Each day I choose to walk in resurrection power is another day free from addiction's grip."

Living in resurrection power means embracing newness of life in everyday decisions:

- Choosing forgiveness when resentment feels justified
- Extending generosity when self-protection seems wiser
- Speaking truth with love when silence would be easier
- Pursuing reconciliation when division seems permanent

Pastor David Thompson explains, "We access resurrection power through the ordinary means of grace—Scripture reading, prayer, worship, communion, and community. These aren't magical practices, but they're the channels through which the Spirit makes resurrection life a daily reality."

Reflection: In what specific area of your life do you most need to experience resurrection power today? What practical step can you take to embrace that power?

Resurrection as Assurance of Eternal Life

The resurrection of Christ provides believers with absolute assurance of eternal life. As Jesus declared, those who believe in Him, even though they physically die, shall live forever spiritually and ultimately physically, at His return (John 11:25).

Helen witnessed this truth when her husband James died after fifty years of marriage. "Standing by his hospital bed, I saw peace in his eyes despite the pain," she recalls. "His last words to me were, 'I'll see you again—this isn't goodbye.' The resurrection turned what could have been unbearable grief into temporary separation with certain reunion."

This promise of resurrection gives meaning to our present sufferings. When Jennifer received a terminal cancer diagnosis at age 35, she told her church, "I'm not afraid of dying. I'm just sad about leaving my children. But because of the resurrection, I know my story doesn't end with a funeral. It continues in God's presence until He resurrects all things."

The resurrection also connects directly to the incarnation we'll explore in the next chapter. Christ's physical body was truly raised—not as a ghost or spiritual entity, but as a glorified physical reality. This affirms the goodness of our physical existence and God's intention to redeem not just our souls but our bodies as well.

Reflection: How would your perspective on death change if you fully embraced the reality of resurrection? How might this change how you live today?

Resurrection as the Foundation of Hope

Resurrection provides unshakable hope amidst life's challenges. Unlike worldly optimism, biblical hope anchored in resurrection is certain, stable, and eternal.

When eighteen-year-old Michael was paralyzed in a car accident, despair threatened to overwhelm him. "I questioned everything," he says. "But eventually, I realized the resurrection promises that this broken body is temporary. One day, I'll have a restored body that works perfectly. That hope gets me through the hardest days."

Similarly, those working in seemingly hopeless situations draw strength from resurrection hope. Dr. Lisa Chen, serving in a war-torn region, explains, "When you're surrounded by death and destruction daily, resurrection hope isn't abstract theology—it's essential survival. It reminds us that evil and suffering don't have the final word."

Resurrection hope transforms how we view seemingly
intractable problems:

- Environmental degradation points us toward the promise
  of creation's renewal

- Systemic injustice reminds us of God's coming perfect
  kingdom

- Incurable diseases heighten our longing for resurrected
  bodies

- Broken relationships anticipate complete restoration

Reflection: What situation in your life or in the world seems
most hopeless? How does resurrection hope specifically address
that situation?

Resurrection and the Community of Faith

The resurrection powerfully shapes community life within
the Church. Believers share a common identity as participants in
Christ's death and resurrection, fostering unity, solidarity, and
mutual care.

At Grace Community Church, this plays out when members
gather around families facing loss. When the Martinez family lost
their home in a fire, the congregation didn't just offer prayers—
they provided temporary housing, replaced essential items, and
helped rebuild. As Pastor Elaine notes, "Resurrection community
means we enter each other's tombs of suffering and help roll away
stones of despair."

The early church in Acts demonstrated this resurrection community daily—sharing possessions, caring for widows and orphans, transcending social barriers, and facing persecution with supernatural joy. Today's church continues this witness when it embodies resurrection life through:

- Radical hospitality that welcomes the stranger
- Economic sharing that addresses inequality
- Reconciliation efforts that heal historic divisions
- Creation care that anticipates cosmic renewal

This community aspect of resurrection connects to both the Trinity (showing how divine community creates human community) and the incarnation (demonstrating how spiritual reality must take tangible, physical form).

Reflection: How is your church community demonstrating resurrection life? What one practice could strengthen your church's witness to resurrection reality?

Resurrection – A Call to Response

Finally, resurrection demands a personal response. Jesus asks each individual believer, "Do you believe this?" This question requires reflection and decision, compelling each person to embrace resurrection not merely as a doctrinal truth but as a personal, transformative reality.

Carlos, a business executive, describes his moment of decision: "I had intellectual belief in the resurrection, but it wasn't changing how I lived. During a Holy Week service, I realized I was living as if this world was all that mattered. That night, I surrendered my career, finances, and future to the risen Christ. Everything changed—not my circumstances, but my perspective on them."

Belief in resurrection invites a dynamic, living relationship with the risen Christ. It means:

- Facing each morning with expectancy for God's life-giving work
- Approaching problems with confidence in resurrection solutions
- Viewing people through the lens of their resurrection potential
- Making decisions in light of eternal rather than temporal values

As we conclude this chapter and prepare to explore Christ's incarnation, remember that resurrection and incarnation are inseparable truths. The incarnate Christ—God in human flesh—conquered death through resurrection, guaranteeing our own future resurrection.

Final Reflections

1. How does understanding Christ's resurrection change your daily perspective on life's challenges?

2. In what practical ways can you demonstrate resurrection hope in your relationships and community?

3. How does believing in Christ's resurrection impact your view of death and eternal life?

4. What one step will you take this week to live more fully in resurrection reality?

6

Incarnation

God in Flesh, God in Us

✦

And the Word become flesh and dwelt among us, and we have seen his glory, glory as of the only Son from the Father, full of grace and truth.

John 1:14 (ESV)

The Radical Significance of God Becoming Human

The doctrine of the incarnation proclaims the profound mystery that God became human in Jesus Christ. The term "incarnation," derived from the Latin word "carne," literally means "in flesh." This teaching asserts that the eternal Word of God took on human form, fully experiencing the reality of human life, yet without compromising His divine nature. John's Gospel vividly captures this profound truth, declaring, "The Word became flesh and dwelt among us" (John 1:14).

This truth is transformative because it means God entered human history as one of us, not merely as an observer or distant deity. God's choice to become incarnate emphasizes His profound identification and solidarity with humanity. Jesus experienced everything common to humanity—pain, temptation, hunger, sorrow—yet remained sinless. The letter to the Hebrews affirms this: "For we do not have a high priest who is unable to sympathize with our weaknesses, but one who in every respect has been tempted as we are, yet without sin" (Hebrews 4:15). He walked perfectly in our human shoes to redeem us completely.

The incarnation powerfully reverses humanity's trajectory initiated by Adam's sin. As Paul describes Jesus as the "last Adam" (1 Corinthians 15:45), Christ undoes the destructive power of original sin. Paul elaborates on this comparison: "For as by a man came death, by a man has come also the resurrection of the dead. For as in Adam all die, so also in Christ shall all be made alive" (1 Corinthians 15:21-22). Through His sinless incarnation, Christ brings divine reconciliation, overcoming death and granting eternal life to all who believe in Him.

Historical Development of the Doctrine

The church's understanding of the incarnation developed over centuries, with significant debates about Christ's nature leading to crucial theological definitions. In the early centuries, various interpretations emerged that either overemphasized Christ's divinity at the expense of His humanity (Docetism) or His humanity at the expense of His divinity (Arianism).

The Council of Nicaea (325 AD) affirmed Christ as "of the same substance" (homoousios) with the Father, establishing His full divinity. Later, the Council of Chalcedon (451 AD) formulated what became the orthodox understanding of Christ's nature as one person with two natures—fully divine and fully human—that exist "without confusion, without change, without division, without separation."

These careful formulations weren't merely academic exercises but vital clarifications that preserved the essence of the gospel message. If Christ were not fully God, He could not save humanity; if He were not fully human, He could not represent humanity. As Gregory of Nazianzus famously stated, "What has not been assumed has not been healed"—affirming that Christ had to fully assume human nature to fully redeem it.

Emmanuel: God With Us

Isaiah prophesied that the Messiah would be named Emmanuel, meaning "God with us" (Isaiah 7:14). This name is profoundly significant as it encapsulates the essence of the incarnation—God drawing near to His creation in intimate relationship. Matthew's Gospel explicitly connects Jesus to this prophecy: "All this took place to fulfill what the Lord had spoken by the prophet: 'Behold, the virgin shall conceive and bear a son, and they shall call his name Emmanuel' (which means, God with us)" (Matthew 1:22-23).

Emmanuel is not just a name but a promise fulfilled. It speaks of God's presence amid humanity's brokenness. Unlike other religious traditions, Christianity uniquely proclaims a God who not only speaks from afar but who actively participates in human suffering. The incarnation demonstrates God's relentless pursuit of humanity, choosing vulnerability and humility to restore a fractured relationship.

This concept of "God with us" builds upon the Jewish understanding of God's presence in the tabernacle and temple, but with a radical new dimension. As John's Gospel declares, Jesus "tabernacled" among us (John 1:14)—using language that would have reminded Jewish readers of God's dwelling in the tabernacle. But now, rather than dwelling in a building, God dwells in human form, making His presence more immediate and personal than ever before.

Thus, Emmanuel transforms our understanding of divine love and intimacy. Through the incarnation, God assures us of His ongoing presence, His unending compassion, and His unwavering commitment to redeem humanity fully. This assurance profoundly shapes how believers perceive their relationship with God and others.

Fully God and Fully Human

Early church theologians, wrestling with the mystery of the incarnation, affirmed Christ's dual nature: fully divine and fully human. This doctrine underscores that in Christ, divinity and humanity coexist perfectly and inseparably. Jesus was not merely a divine being disguised in human form nor a human elevated to divine status; He was genuinely both at once.

Philippians 2:5-11 beautifully captures this mystery, describing how Christ, "though he was in the form of God, did not count equality with God a thing to be grasped, but emptied himself, by taking the form of a servant, being born in the likeness of men." This passage shows both the pre-existence of Christ as divine and His willing assumption of full humanity.

This dual nature is critical because it validates Christ's unique capacity to mediate between humanity and God. As fully divine, He has the authority and power to forgive sins and grant eternal life. As fully human, He genuinely experiences human limitations, making Him a sympathetic and authentic mediator who understands our weaknesses (Hebrews 4:15).

Different Christian traditions have emphasized various aspects of this mystery. Eastern Orthodox theology particularly celebrates how the incarnation divinizes humanity ("theosis"), while Western traditions often emphasize how it enables atonement. Reformed theologians highlight how it fulfills God's covenant promises, while Pentecostal traditions may focus on how it demonstrates God's desire for intimate relationship with humanity. These diverse perspectives enrich our understanding of this profound mystery.

Recognizing Jesus as fully God and fully human deepens our worship and devotion. It encourages believers that they worship a God who intimately understands human struggles yet retains the power to redeem and transform them completely. This doctrine profoundly shapes discipleship, emphasizing dependence on a compassionate and powerful Savior.

The Perfect Sacrifice

The incarnation was necessary for God's justice and mercy to coexist harmoniously. Humanity's sinfulness warranted divine judgment, but God's profound mercy compelled a redemptive solution. Only a perfect sacrifice could satisfy divine justice and offer mercy simultaneously. Jesus, God incarnate, was uniquely positioned to fulfill this requirement.

Christ's sinless life qualified Him as the perfect substitute, bearing humanity's punishment on the cross. He became the sacrificial lamb, ensuring God's judgment was satisfied, thus granting believers access to God's mercy. Through the incarnation, God effectively resolved the tension between His righteousness and compassion without compromising either.

The letter to the Hebrews elaborates on this theme: "Therefore he had to be made like his brothers in every respect, so that he might become a merciful and faithful high priest in the service of God, to make propitiation for the sins of the people" (Hebrews 2:17). The incarnation was not an end in itself but a necessary step in God's redemptive plan.

This understanding should lead believers to profound gratitude and humility. It demonstrates the immense value God places on humanity, motivating believers to pursue holiness and reflect Christ's sacrificial love in daily life. The incarnation vividly portrays God's redemptive strategy and divine love, inviting deep worship and reverent devotion.

The Incarnation and Resurrection: Fulfilling Redemption

Building on the previous chapter's focus on resurrection, we see how the incarnation and resurrection function as complementary doctrines in God's redemptive plan. The incarnation initiated Christ's redemptive work by joining divine nature with human nature, while the resurrection completed and validated this work by conquering death.

Through the incarnation, Christ identified with humanity's weakness and mortality; through the resurrection, He transformed that mortality into immortality. As Paul writes, "For as by a man came death, by a man has come also the resurrection of the dead" (1 Corinthians 15:21). The same physical body that was born in Bethlehem and died on Calvary was raised to new life, demonstrating that God's redemption includes the physical dimension of existence.

Together, these doctrines affirm that God values material creation and physical existence. The incarnation declares that physicality isn't inherently evil or inferior to spirituality, while the resurrection promises the redemption and transformation of our physical existence. This holistic redemption prepares us for understanding the coming chapter on New Creation.

Continuing Incarnation Through the Church

Significantly, the incarnation did not conclude with Christ's ascension but continues through the church. Jesus's physical presence ascended, yet His presence remains active in believers through the Holy Spirit. Collectively, the church embodies

Christ's presence on earth, becoming His hands and feet, ministering compassion, justice, and redemption.

Paul describes the church as "the body of Christ" (1 Corinthians 12:27), an expression that goes beyond metaphor to describe the church's role in continuing Christ's incarnational presence. He even makes the startling claim that the church is "the fullness of him who fills all in all" (Ephesians 1:23), suggesting that Christ's presence is manifested through His people.

Thus, the church's mission is fundamentally incarnational. Believers continue Christ's work of reconciliation, healing, and transformation within communities and across cultures. The ongoing incarnation emphasizes believers' responsibility to authentically reflect Christ in every sphere, bridging gaps between God and humanity.

Practically, this means believers must engage their contexts with incarnational intentionality, embracing humility, vulnerability, and active service. The church, embodying Christ's ongoing incarnation, must represent God's tangible presence in the world, faithfully proclaiming and demonstrating the transformative gospel message.

Incarnation and Daily Discipleship

Understanding the incarnation deeply influences discipleship, profoundly shaping believers' relationships with God and others. Recognizing Christ as Emmanuel inspires believers to practice God's presence daily, nurturing a vibrant spiritual life through prayer, reflection, and compassionate living. Believers are invited to cultivate an incarnational spirituality that echoes Christ's humility and empathy.

This practice fosters deeper relationships, encourages authenticity in interactions, and compels believers toward active social engagement. It transforms ordinary activities into sacred acts, highlighting God's presence in everyday moments. Thus, believers learn to view themselves and others through incarnational lenses, continually shaped by Christ's example.

Incarnation in a Digital Age

In our contemporary digital world, the doctrine of incarnation speaks powerfully to how Christians should navigate virtual environments. The incarnation reminds us that physical presence matters—God chose to enter humanity not as a disembodied voice or message but as a person with a body.

While digital tools enable connection across distances, an incarnational perspective reminds believers to value and prioritize physical presence when possible. The temptation to substitute digital interaction for physical community should be resisted, as human flourishing requires embodied relationships that engage all senses.

However, digital tools can serve incarnational purposes when physical presence isn't possible. Video calls with the homebound, online communities for the isolated, and digital resources for the underserved can extend Christ's presence to those otherwise disconnected. The key is to ensure that technology serves incarnational values rather than replacing them.

As believers navigate between physical and virtual spaces, the incarnation calls them to bring authentic, holistic presence to every interaction—whether physical or digital—sharing Christ's love across all dimensions of human experience.

The Incarnation and New Creation

Looking forward to the next chapter on New Creation, the incarnation provides a theological foundation for understanding God's ultimate intentions for creation. By taking on human flesh, God demonstrated that His redemptive plan includes the material world, not just human souls.

The incarnation reveals that God values creation enough to enter into it and experience it from within. This divine affirmation of creation's goodness points toward its ultimate renewal rather than its abandonment. The resurrected Christ, with His glorified yet physical body, gives us a glimpse of this renewed creation.

As we will explore in the next chapter, the God who became incarnate in Jesus Christ will ultimately bring about a new heaven and new earth where He will dwell with His people forever, fulfilling the promise of Emmanuel—God with us—in its most complete form.

Reflection Questions

1. How does knowing Christ as "God with us" shape your daily interactions with God and others?

2. In what ways does Jesus's full humanity provide comfort or encouragement in your struggles?

3. Consider the historical development of the doctrine of incarnation. Why do you think it was so important for the early church to clarify Christ's nature as fully God and fully human?

4. How does the ongoing incarnation through the church affect your view of your role within your community?

5. How might the doctrine of incarnation inform your use of digital technology and social media?

6. What connection do you see between Christ's incarnation and the promise of resurrection and new creation?

7. What practical steps can you take to embody incarnational living in your daily routines and relationships?

8. How can you better reflect the humility and compassion of Christ in your interactions with those around you?

7

New Creation

Born Again to Live Again

✦

Therefore, if anyone is in Christ, the new creation has come: The old has gone, the new is here!

2 Corinthians 5:17 (NIV)

Becoming Who God Intended

B eing a new creation means embracing God's original intent for humanity. Just as God created Adam and Eve in His image and likeness, becoming a new creation restores us to that original, divine intention. Sin distorted God's image in humanity, but through Christ's redemptive work, the distorted image is realigned and perfected. To be born again is not merely a spiritual metaphor; it is a transformative event, a second genesis, signaling that something entirely new and divine has begun within us.

In John 3:3, Jesus explicitly says to Nicodemus, "Very truly I tell you, no one can see the kingdom of God unless they are born again." This rebirth is not symbolic; it represents a complete transformation of our spiritual identity. The old nature shaped by sin and worldly influences gives way to a new, regenerated nature shaped by the Spirit of God.

> **Consider This:** How does this understanding of new creation build upon Christ's incarnation? Just as God took on human flesh in Jesus, now His Spirit dwells within believers, continuing the incarnational pattern.

This process doesn't eliminate our unique personalities or human experiences but transforms them, aligning them with God's purposes. Consider Sarah, a naturally outspoken person who previously used her voice to tear others down. After becoming a new creation, her boldness remains, but now she advocates for the vulnerable and speaks truth in love.

Our new identity as God's children compels us to live differently. Understanding who we are in Christ affects every aspect of our daily lives, from how we view ourselves and others to how we interact within our communities. It restores dignity and worth not only in ourselves but also in how we treat others, emphasizing unity and love across social, racial, and cultural divides.

Regeneration and Spiritual Rebirth

Regeneration is the theological term describing our spiritual rebirth. It involves more than moral improvement or intellectual enlightenment; regeneration is a supernatural act by which the Holy Spirit imparts new life. This rebirth reconnects our spirit with God's Spirit, reanimating us spiritually and enabling us to live in true fellowship with God. As Christ was incarnated, God's Spirit now incarnates within us, making us truly new beings.

Paul beautifully captures this in Titus 3:5, "He saved us, not because of righteous things we had done, but because of his mercy. He saved us through the washing of rebirth and renewal by the Holy Spirit." Notice the terms 'washing' and 'renewal'—they reflect a comprehensive cleansing and radical reorientation toward God. Regeneration purges our spiritual corruption, implants divine nature within, and sets the foundation for ongoing transformation.

This spiritual rebirth is both instant and ongoing. While regeneration occurs at the moment of faith in Christ, its effects permeate throughout our entire lives. It initiates a continuous journey of sanctification, reshaping our hearts, desires, and actions according to God's original design.

Personal Application: Take a moment to reflect on areas in your life where you still operate from your old identity. What would it look like to approach these areas from your regenerated identity in Christ?

Baptism—Symbol and Reality

While water baptism itself does not cause regeneration, it profoundly symbolizes the spiritual reality of rebirth. Baptism acts as a tangible representation of the transformation from death into new life. Going underwater symbolizes dying to the old self, and emerging from the water symbolizes rising into a new life in Christ. This mirrors our spiritual journey, aligning with Romans 6:4, "We were therefore buried with him through baptism into death in order that, just as Christ was raised from the dead… we too may live a new life."

Yet, the reality it symbolizes is even deeper. Baptism, performed within the community of faith, symbolizes our collective participation in Christ's death and resurrection. It is not merely individual; it situates believers within the ongoing incarnation of Christ through the Church.

David's experience illustrates this communal dimension. After years of private faith, his public baptism was witnessed by his church family. Afterward, an elderly member approached him, saying, "Now we're family. Your struggles are our struggles, and our strengths are your strengths." This interaction transformed David's understanding of faith from a private journey to a shared pilgrimage.

Baptism proclaims publicly that we belong to a community born anew by the Spirit. Practically, baptism also reminds us regularly of our new identity, continuously encouraging us to live out this transformed existence in the everyday.

Living in Newness of Life

Being born again brings new perspectives, desires, and abilities. Our transformation should influence how we live each day. Paul encourages believers to "walk in newness of life" (Romans 6:4). Walking in this new life involves active, practical steps—abandoning old patterns of behavior and embracing new spiritual disciplines. It means aligning our lives to reflect God's holiness and righteousness consistently.

Practical Steps:

- Begin each day acknowledging your identity in Christ through prayer

- Replace habits of negative self-talk with scriptural truths about your new nature

- Identify one relationship where you can demonstrate Christ-like love this week

- Schedule regular times for Scripture meditation on passages about new life in Christ

- Join a small group where you can discuss your journey of transformation

Each step toward holiness, even small ones, represents the power of Christ's resurrection at work within us. The more we lean into our regenerated identity, the more naturally we reflect Christ's character in our relationships, decisions, and daily interactions. This continual transformation marks the ongoing work of the Spirit in believers.

Marina, a business executive, demonstrates this principle. Previously known for ruthless efficiency, after embracing her new identity in Christ, she began intentionally mentoring younger employees and bringing ethical considerations into business discussions. These small changes gradually transformed her leadership style and company culture, revealing Christ's character in her professional sphere.

Old Challenges, New Power

Though reborn, believers often still face familiar struggles and temptations. However, regeneration equips us to face these challenges with new power—the indwelling Holy Spirit. While the presence of temptation remains, our response to it is transformed. Galatians 5:16 reminds us, "Walk by the Spirit, and you will not gratify the desires of the flesh." This power is not merely about resisting sin but positively embracing righteousness.

When confronted with old habits or sinful tendencies, we now respond not by mere human effort but by reliance on God's transformative Spirit. Consider these practical responses to common struggles:

1. When facing anger: Rather than suppressing or exploding in rage, pause to invite the Spirit's peace and ask how this situation can be addressed in love.

2. When experiencing anxiety: Instead of becoming consumed by worry, acknowledge your limited control and actively entrust the situation to God's care.

3. When confronting addiction: Rather than cycling between indulgence and shame, seek support from trusted believers and practice disciplines that strengthen your spiritual identity.

This daily dependence on the Spirit's power is crucial in maintaining our new creation identity, continually enabling victory over sin and temptation.

Community of New Creations

Our identity as new creations is not solitary. We are born again into the family of God—the Church, the Body of Christ. This communal aspect is essential, as it reflects the incarnational nature of our rebirth. As Christ's incarnation was the physical manifestation of God, the Church is now the collective incarnation of Christ, continually living out His purposes in the world.

Being part of this new community involves mutual support, accountability, and shared mission. Acts 2:42–47 provides a model, highlighting devotion to teaching, fellowship, communal meals, prayer, and generosity. As a community of new creations, we are called to model unity, love, and justice, actively representing Christ in our local and global contexts.

> **Navigating Community Challenges:** Even as new creations, church communities face difficulties. When conflict arises, our new identity calls us to reconciliation rather than division. When differences in doctrine or practice emerge, we're called to unity in essentials and grace in non-essentials. When a brother or sister falls into sin, our response should be restoration rather than rejection.

The Riverside Church's story exemplifies this. When their community was split over a controversial issue, rather than separating, they established listening circles where members shared their perspectives with genuine openness. This process, grounded in their shared identity in Christ, eventually led to a deeper unity despite continued differences of opinion.

This communal dimension of our new creation identity serves as a foretaste of the eschatological reality we anticipate— where all of creation will be made new and God's people will live in perfect harmony.

Eternal Perspective

Lastly, becoming a new creation fundamentally shifts our perspective toward eternity. Our rebirth not only changes our present reality but reorients our hearts toward the future promises of God. This eternal perspective shapes our daily priorities, helping us discern what truly matters in God's kingdom. Colossians 3:1–2 instructs, "Set your hearts on things above...not on earthly things."

Living with an eternal perspective encourages us to invest in relationships, service, and actions that have lasting significance. It instills hope, providing strength to endure present struggles, knowing that our new life in Christ will ultimately culminate in eternal fellowship with God.

> **Connecting to Eschatology:** Our identity as new creations points forward to the complete renewal of all things promised in Revelation 21:5, "I am making everything new!" The transformation we experience now is a foretaste of the cosmic restoration to come. In this way, our personal regeneration connects directly to God's ultimate plan for all creation.

When Helen received a terminal diagnosis, her response astonished her doctors. Rather than despair, she spoke of her remaining time as "preparation for the greater life to come." Her eternal perspective, rooted in her identity as a new creation, transformed what could have been a time of bitterness into a powerful witness of hope that influenced dozens around her.

Reflection and Application

1. **Personal Reflection:** How does recognizing yourself as a new creation change your daily decisions? Identify one area where you need to more fully embrace your new identity.

2. **Practical Application:** What specific spiritual habit can you implement this week to walk more intentionally in this newness of life?

3. **Community Engagement:** How can you strengthen your participation in the community of faith to better reflect your identity as part of Christ's ongoing incarnation in the world?

4. **Eternal Mindset:** In what ways might your priorities change if you consistently viewed your daily choices through an eternal lens?

For Further Study:

- Explore 2 Corinthians 5:11-21 for Paul's complete teaching on new creation
- Read John 1:12-13 alongside John 3 to deepen your understanding of spiritual rebirth
- Consider how Ezekiel's vision of dry bones (Ezekiel 37) foreshadows the concept of regeneration

8

Eschatology

Living in Light of the End

✛

Therefore, keep watch, because you do not know on what day your Lord will come.

Matthew 24:42 (NIV)

Understanding Christ's Return

E schatology, the doctrine concerning the "last things," teaches us that the redemptive work initiated by Christ at His incarnation and continued through our regeneration as new creations will reach its ultimate fulfillment in His return. The return of Christ is not merely a footnote of Christian belief; it is central to our hope and daily discipleship. Scripture assures us that Jesus, our resurrected Lord, will return visibly, triumphantly, and personally (Acts 1:11). This doctrine underscores that history is purposeful, not random—moving inevitably toward the Kingdom's consummation, where Christ will reign forever with His Church.

This return signifies more than escape or relief; it means the final restoration of all creation under God's perfect rule (Revelation 21:1-4). In this consummated Kingdom, death, sorrow, injustice, and evil are abolished, and God's reign is established eternally. Therefore, believers look forward not just to escape the troubles of this world but actively participate in Christ's kingdom work until He comes.

Understanding Christ's imminent return shapes our perspective and engagement in this present age. It encourages believers to persevere through trials, live righteously, and pursue holiness. Our daily decisions and priorities become infused with the significance of eternity, reflecting that every moment counts toward the ultimate revelation of God's glory.

Application: Consider how your weekly schedule reflects your belief in Christ's return. Which activities might you adjust to better align with kingdom priorities? Take time this week to evaluate one area where your time investment doesn't reflect your eternal values.

Eschatological Perspectives Across Christian Traditions

Throughout church history, Christians have understood the details of Christ's return differently while maintaining the core hope of His coming again. Eastern Orthodox traditions emphasize the transformative presence of the future Kingdom breaking into the present through liturgy and sacraments. Roman Catholic teaching highlights the already-present Kingdom in the Eucharist while anticipating its future perfection. Protestant denominations range from premillennial views (Christ returns before establishing a thousand-year reign), to amillennial perspectives (the millennium represents Christ's current spiritual reign), to postmillennial beliefs (the gospel gradually transforms the world before Christ's return).

Despite these differences, all major Christian traditions affirm Jesus's personal return, the resurrection of believers, final judgment, and eternal life with God. Rather than allowing different interpretations to divide us, understanding these perspectives can enrich our appreciation for the multi-faceted hope we share in Christ's return.

Application: When discussing end-times beliefs with Christians who hold different views, focus first on your shared hope in Christ's return before addressing differences. Practice saying, "Though we may see the details differently, we both eagerly await our Lord's coming."

Hope as a Transformative Power

The Christian hope anchored in Christ's return is transformative. Unlike worldly optimism, biblical hope is grounded in the certainty of God's promises fulfilled through Jesus Christ. This hope sustains us amid present difficulties, reminding us that suffering and injustice do not have the final word. It strengthens us to resist despair, complacency, and worldly distractions, empowering us instead to live purposefully and passionately for God's Kingdom.

This eschatological hope also compels us to advocate and embody justice, mercy, and peace today. It is not passive; it actively transforms how we engage with social and communal realities. Just as Francis Grimké courageously addressed racial injustices from the pulpit in the late 19th and early 20th centuries, believers throughout history have been moved by eschatological hope to oppose slavery, establish hospitals, combat human trafficking, and seek justice for the oppressed. We too are called to demonstrate gospel fidelity in societal spheres, anticipating the just and redemptive Kingdom Christ will bring in its fullness.

Practically, this hope urges us to live in constant readiness, mirroring the vigilance and expectancy of the earliest Christian communities. Believers are motivated not by fear but by joy and anticipation, embodying a life marked by gratitude, generosity, and kingdom-focused living.

Application: Identify one area of injustice or suffering in your community. Take a concrete step this month to address it in a way that reflects the coming Kingdom's values of justice, compassion, and restoration.

Personal Eschatology: Our Individual Journey's End

While we await Christ's cosmic return, each believer faces a "personal eschatology"—our individual encounter with the Lord at death. Jesus told the thief on the cross, "Today you will be with me in paradise" (Luke 23:43), giving us confidence that believers immediately enter Christ's presence upon death, even as we await the final resurrection of our bodies. This personal dimension of eschatology reminds us that preparation for meeting the Lord is not a distant concern but an immediate reality that should shape our daily lives.

The reality of our mortality does not contradict our hope in Christ's return but rather intensifies our desire to live faithfully now. As the Puritan Richard Baxter wrote, "Live as if you were going to die tomorrow, and yet as if you were going to live a thousand years." Our personal end magnifies the importance of using each day to grow in Christlikeness and faithful service.

Application: Write a brief reflection on how you would like to be remembered after your life ends. What spiritual legacies and kingdom investments are you currently making that will outlast your earthly life?

Balanced Engagement with End Times Teaching

Scripture calls us to attentive watchfulness regarding Christ's return without becoming obsessed with predicting its timing or details. Throughout history, some believers have fallen into unhealthy extremes—either becoming so fixated on eschatological timelines and signs that they neglect present discipleship, or so disinterested in Christ's return that they live with little reference to our ultimate hope.

Jesus himself warned against calculating specific dates (Matthew 24:36) while still emphasizing vigilant preparation (Matthew 25:1-13). Healthy engagement with eschatology maintains this balance: earnestly expecting Christ's return without presuming to know exactly when or how it will unfold. This balanced perspective enables us to live faithfully in the present while maintaining our future hope.

Application: If you find yourself either anxious about end-times events or completely disengaged from thinking about Christ's return, take time to pray for balance. Ask God to help you maintain hopeful expectation without speculation or fear.

Holiness and Active Waiting

Living in the light of eschatology demands holiness. The Apostle Peter instructs believers to lead "holy and godly lives as you look forward to the day of God" (2 Peter 3:11-12). Holiness involves more than moral purity; it encompasses total devotion and alignment to God's purposes. Thus, active waiting is not passive resignation but an engaged pursuit of Christ-likeness, shaped profoundly by the anticipation of His return.

This doctrine emphasizes the urgency of personal and communal transformation. As a community awaiting the Bridegroom, we are called to reflect the character of Christ visibly and authentically, signaling to the world the redemptive reality soon to be fully realized. This pursuit involves prayer, scripture meditation, worship, and righteous living, continually cultivating a lifestyle ready for Christ's return.

In practical terms, holiness in light of eschatology guides our everyday ethics and interactions. We become people who forgive readily, serve sacrificially, and witness boldly, not as acts of religious duty but as heartfelt responses to the imminent return of our Lord.

Application: Consider one relationship in which you need to practice forgiveness or reconciliation. Take action this week, recognizing that living "ready" for Christ's return means maintaining peace and love in our relationships.

Justice and Kingdom Ethics

Eschatological living inherently embraces the ethics of God's coming Kingdom. The return of Christ is the ultimate act of divine justice, overturning every injustice, oppression, and corruption. This expectation instructs believers to be proactive agents of kingdom justice today. We become advocates for the marginalized, echoing the prophetic calls to righteousness and justice throughout Scripture.

Historically, Christians moved by eschatological urgency have catalyzed significant social reforms. William Wilberforce's persistence in abolishing the British slave trade was sustained by his belief in Christ's coming judgment. Dietrich Bonhoeffer's resistance to Nazi tyranny flowed from his conviction about God's ultimate rule. Following in this legacy, we too must engage actively in our communities, reflecting the just character of our coming King. Our societal involvement—shaped by a clear understanding of Christ's return—signals our anticipation of the fully restored creation.

Thus, kingdom ethics is not optional; it's central to our discipleship. It requires courage, clarity, and compassion, qualities exemplified in Christ and echoed profoundly in the ministries of historical figures like Francis Grimké. In practicing these ethics, we vividly demonstrate our commitment to Christ's lordship and our expectation of His imminent return.

Application: Research a justice issue that aligns with your gifts and calling. Commit to regular prayer about this issue and identify one tangible action you can take to address it in the coming month.

Unity in Anticipation

Eschatology fosters unity within the Church by reminding us of our shared destiny in Christ. Paul's epistles emphasize unity as integral to Christian identity and witness (Ephesians 4:3-6). As believers awaiting Christ's return, we are compelled to overcome divisions and conflicts, seeking reconciliation and harmony reflective of our ultimate reconciliation in Christ.

While Christians may differ on eschatological details, our fundamental hope remains the same—we eagerly await Christ's return and the full establishment of His kingdom. These differences need not divide us. Instead, they can enrich our understanding through respectful dialogue and mutual learning. When we focus on our shared hope rather than disputed details, we demonstrate the unifying power of Christ's return.

This unity is both a testimony to the world and a source of encouragement within the Church. Together, as one body, we affirm our collective hope and mission, bolstering one another in the journey toward Christ's return. Practically, this unity influences how we interact, resolve conflicts, and collaborate in ministry and mission, always mindful that our unity testifies powerfully to the reality of Christ's impending return.

Application: If you have experienced division with fellow believers over end-times views, take initiative to restore fellowship by acknowledging your shared hope in Christ's return while respecting different perspectives on secondary details.

Proclaiming the Gospel Until He Comes

The imminent return of Christ compels urgent evangelistic engagement. Believers are tasked with sharing the gospel passionately and persistently, knowing that each moment brings us closer to the ultimate consummation. This urgency does not incite fear-based evangelism but encourages grace-filled, authentic proclamation of Christ's redeeming love.

Eschatology propels the Church into proactive mission, acknowledging that time is short, and souls are valuable. This mission mindset energizes believers, spurring innovative, compassionate, and courageous gospel outreach. It also calls for practical discipleship and mentorship within the Church, equipping believers to effectively communicate their faith in light of Christ's imminent return.

As we conclude our exploration of essential Christian doctrines, we recognize that eschatology brings all other doctrines to their fullest expression. Christ's deity ensures His triumph; our understanding of original sin heightens our appreciation for final redemption; Scripture guides our understanding of last things; the Trinity will be fully revealed and experienced; the resurrection will be universal; the incarnation's purpose will be fulfilled; and our new creation in Christ will be perfected. In this light, eschatology is not merely the end of our doctrinal journey but the glorious fulfillment of all God has revealed and promised.

Application: Share your hope in Christ's return with someone this week. Rather than focusing on complex timelines or controversial details, emphasize how this hope gives purpose to your daily life and decisions.

Reflection Questions

1. How does the doctrine of eschatology influence your daily life and priorities?

2. What specific actions can you take today to reflect a lifestyle of active waiting and holiness?

3. In what ways can your church community better embody unity and kingdom ethics in anticipation of Christ's return?

4. How does understanding Christ's return encourage you to address injustices around you with greater urgency and compassion?

5. What practical steps can you take to more actively proclaim the gospel and disciple others in anticipation of Christ's imminent return?

6. How does your personal awareness of mortality (personal eschatology) affect how you view Christ's cosmic return?

7. Which Christian traditions different from your own might offer valuable perspectives on eschatology that could enrich your understanding?

8. In what specific ways does your belief in eschatology connect with and complete your understanding of the other seven doctrines we've explored?

Augustine, Saint. *Confessions.* Translated by Henry Chadwick. Oxford University Press, 2009.

Blocher, Henri. *Original Sin: Illuminating the Riddle.* InterVarsity Press, 1999.

Hoekema, Anthony A. *Created in God's Image.* Eerdmans, 1986.

Murray, John. *The Imputation of Adam's Sin.* Presbyterian & Reformed Publishing, 1959.

Canon (Scripture)

Carson, D.A., and John D. Woodbridge, eds. *Scripture and Truth.* Baker Academic, 1992.

Jobes, Karen H., and Moisés Silva. *Invitation to the Septuagint.* 2nd ed. Baker Academic, 2015.

Köstenberger, Andreas J., and Michael J. Kruger. *The Heresy of Orthodoxy.* Crossway, 2010.

Kruger, Michael J. *Canon Revisited: Establishing the Origins and Authority of the New Testament Books.* Crossway, 2012.

Triune Nature of God (Trinity)

Frame, John M. *The Doctrine of God.* P&R Publishing, 2002.

Letham, Robert. *The Holy Trinity: In Scripture, History, Theology, and Worship.* P&R Publishing, 2004.

Sanders, Fred. *The Deep Things of God: How the Trinity Changes Everything.* Crossway, 2010.

Resurrection

Gaffin, Richard B. *Resurrection and Redemption: A Study in Paul's Soteriology.* Presbyterian & Reformed Publishing, 1987.

O'Collins, Gerald. *The Easter Jesus and the Gospel of the Resurrection.* Orbis Books, 2014.

Wright, N.T. *The Resurrection of the Son of God.* Fortress Press, 2003.

Incarnation

Macleod, Donald. *The Person of Christ.* InterVarsity Press, 1998.

Tanner, Kathryn. *Jesus, Humanity and the Trinity: A Brief Systematic Theology.* Fortress Press, 2001.

Torrance, Thomas F. *Incarnation: The Person and Life of Christ.* IVP Academic, 2008.

Wellum, Stephen J. *God the Son Incarnate: The Doctrine of Christ.* Crossway, 2016.

New Creation

Beale, G.K. *A New Testament Biblical Theology.* Baker Academic, 2011.

Middleton, J. Richard. *A New Heaven and a New Earth.* Baker Academic, 2014.

Richter, Sandra. *The Epic of Eden: A Christian Entry into the Old Testament.* IVP Academic, 2008.

Wright, N.T. *Surprised by Hope.* HarperOne, 2008.

Eschatology

Hoekema, Anthony A. *The Bible and the Future.* Eerdmans, 1979.

Poythress, Vern S. *The Returning King: A Guide to the Book of Revelation.* P&R Publishing, 2000.

Riddlebarger, Kim. *A Case for Amillennialism: Understanding the End Times.* Baker Books, 2013.

The African American Christian Experience

Bradley, Anthony B. *Liberating Black Theology.* Crossway, 2010.

Cone, James H. *The Cross and the Lynching Tree.* Orbis Books, 2011.

Emerson, Michael O., and Christian Smith. *Divided by Faith.* Oxford University Press, 2001.

Evans, Tony. *Oneness Embraced.* Moody Publishers, 2015.

McCaulley, Esau. *Reading While Black.* IVP Academic, 2020.

Pierce, Yolanda. *In My Grandmother's House.* Broadleaf Books, 2021.
Thurman, Howard. *Jesus and the Disinherited.* Beacon Press, 1996.

Francis James Grimké's Work

Freeman, Eric J. *Grimké's Gospel Echo: A Handbook for Preaching.* The Freeman Institute for Integrative Research, 2025.

Freeman, Eric J. *Pauline Echoes in the Preaching and Activism of Francis James Grimké (1850–1937).* PhD diss., Anderson University, 2023. ProQuest: https://www.proquest.com/dissertations-theses/pauline-echoes-preaching-activism-francis-james/docview/3155970753/se-2

Grimké, Francis J. *The Works of Francis J. Grimké, Volumes 1–4.* Edited by Carter G. Woodson. Associated Publishers, 1942.

Additional Practical and Mainline Texts

Keller, Timothy. *The Reason for God.* Viking (Penguin), 2008.

Warren, Tish Harrison. *Liturgy of the Ordinary.* IVP Books, 2016.

Wright, N.T. *Simply Christian.* HarperOne, 2006.

Yancey, Philip. *What's So Amazing About Grace?* Zondervan, 1997.

About the Author

Eric J. Freeman, PhD (Homiletics and Social Ethics, Anderson University), MA (Theological Ethics, Lutheran Theological Southern Seminary), BS (Finance, University of Florida), is a scholar-practitioner with over 30 years of ministry experience. As a bishop within the Christian Covenant Fellowship of Ministries and founder and Senior Pastor of The Meeting Place Church of Greater Columbia, he has led the transformation of a 23-acre campus into a vibrant hub for community engagement and social impact.

Dr. Freeman's academic and ministerial work converge in his pioneering development of the Evangelical Emancipatory Homiletics™ framework—a theological and homiletical approach emerging from his decades of pastoral preaching, scholarly reflection, and historical research. His preaching and scholarship critically engage under-examined societal issues through a biblical lens, bridging rigorous theology with practical action and advocacy. Named 2023 Humanitarian of the Year by the South Carolina State Conference of the NAACP, Dr. Freeman embodies a deep commitment to empowering believers to live out gospel truths with integrity, compassion, and social responsibility.

He and his wife, Coleen, are the proud parents of two adult children.

The Freeman Institute

FOR INTEGRATIVE RESEARCH

www.ingramcontent.com/pod-product-compliance
Lightning Source LLC
Chambersburg PA
CBHW021149090426
42740CB00008B/1016